Twelve Bells to Freedom

A FAMILY'S JOURNEY FROM
COMMUNISM TO FREEDOM

THE TRUE-LIFE STORY OF IREN AND LAJOS SUHAJDA'S
FAMILY WALKING IN GOD'S FOOTSTEPS TO FREEDOM.

LASZLO T SUHAJDA

No part of this book may be reproduced, stored in a retrieval system or transmitted to any form or by any means without the prior written permission of the publishers, except by a reviewer who may quote in a review to be printed in a newspaper, magazine, or journal.

TWELVE BELLS to FREEDOM

Copyright © 2023 Laszlo Suhajda

All rights reserved.

ISBN 979-8-218-32844-3 (Paperback)

ISBN 979-8-218-32845-0 (Hardcopy)

The reason I wrote the book.

The Suhajda family's journey from tyranny and oppression to freedom gave a future to my brothers and sister, as well as our children and grandchildren.

Iren and Lajos witnessed and experienced devastation and the love of family. My grandparents were the rock that brought comfort during tragic times and the love to carry on. This is a journey, a dream for a better life where faith and determination can provide security and happiness for all.

I dedicate this book to my mother, Iren Menrath Suhajda, my father Lajos Zoltan Suhajda, my grandparents, Anna and Matyas Menrath, and all of our relatives who stood by my family in times of need.

This book is based on oral history from my parents, tape-recorded by myself in 1973 and 1974.

Laszlo Suhajda
Author

TESTIMONIAL

I met Laszlo Suhajda through stage32.com, and we became good friends. He told me about TWELVE BELLS TO FREEDOM, his family's story, and I could hardly wait to read it.

It is a family's life journey with unique perspectives during a dark time in world history, during World War II, Russia's postwar occupation of Hungary, blacklists, and efforts to eliminate religious freedoms. Their journey covers every emotion with the determination for a better life.

I recommend this book to people who like true stories. It would be appealing to historians, readers who like family and faith-related books, and the younger generation, who can learn about communism.

This is a courageous, gripping, dramatic story that holds your attention and provides an insight into life under communism.

Sincerely,

Elaine Elizabeth Presley

Author
KID OF THE KING

Table of Contents

Chapter 1   1
Family History

Chapter 2   6
Borgond

Chapter 3   17
Jewish Deportation Borgond

Chapter 4   29
End of WWII

Chapter 5   37
Civilian Life

Chapter 6   49
Turbulent Times

Chapter 7   59
The Trial

Chapter 8   63
From Hard Times, To Family

Chapter 9   68
Államvédelmi Hatóság, AVH

Chapter 10   70
Hungarian Revolution

Chapter 11 77
    The Escape
References 98

Author's Bio 102

Chapter 1

Family History

Author: Laszlo T. Suhajda

I, Iren Menrath, was born on April 29, 1928, in the City of Versetz, during the Austrian and Hungarian monarchy. After World War 1, Hungary was divided up as punishment for WWI. Hungary was separated from Austria through a redistricting of Hungary, which was known as the Trianon Treaty in 1920. The City of Versetz was Hungarian but after redistricting it became part of Yugoslavia.

Matyas Menrath, my father, was born in 1885. He started working for the railroad in 1910, and in 1920 we lived in Versetz. My father could not believe a Hungarian city would be given to Yugoslavia as punishment for WWI. He believed the responsibility fell upon the Germans who started WWI. My family was a religious family. We attended church and prayed during dinner for the blessings we had. This faith proved to be the strength we relied on through all of our hardships of life. My childhood started in Versets. I was the youngest of four siblings. My sister Anna was 10 years older, and her nickname was Nuci. I had two brothers, Nandor and Lajos. Lajos was my half-brother and the oldest, and he went by his middle name Janos, with the nickname Jani. He was 14 years older than me. Matyas, my father, had a first wife who died of tuberculosis, and he married my mother, Anna Bittlingmayer. My second brother Ferdinand, nicknamed Feri, lived in the

Iren Menrath 3 years old, home photo

village of Godisa. The neighbors and friends called him Nandi. He was 12 years older than I. They were loving and gave me direction through their example.

As I was growing up, I observed my older brothers and sister and learned from their experiences how to live my life. My sister, Nuci, got married when I was just 10 years old. I was raised as an only child, with a happy childhood. Everything was family-oriented, with family dinners and discussions, prayers before every meal, and a strong family base with an emphasis on right and wrong. My mother, Anna, was a housewife and very supportive to all her children. She kept the household organized, took care of all the cooking, gardening, listened to our worries and concerns and gave us a hug when we were sad. She was influential with my father and her recommendations were respected.

Iren family photo, back row, Jani, Nuci, Feri. Front row Anna, Iren, and Matyas

My father ran the railroad station in Versets. He handled all aspects from general to technical. He sold tickets and received telegrams with order requests to inspect areas of the rails. His technical experience made him a very respected and important worker. He was the go-to railroad man and was counted on when something was needed. As a young boy, he learned responsibility early. Upon returning from school one day his mother, with tears in her eyes, hugged him and told him his father had died. He had died of a heart attack. My father was 14 years old, and he became the head of the household! He was responsible for the care of his sister, two brothers and mother. So, he quit school and worked hard to support his family.

We lived in Kisgombos, a Hungarian village, in Yugoslavia which was called Bogojavo Selo. I became aware of the world around me and had friends who were Hungarian, Yugoslavian, and German. I played with a German neighbor boy named Jozsi. I was about 4 years old and was living a happy childhood. A neighbor man named Lenjel Bachi spent time with my friends and me, and he called me his little Chickadee. My brother, Jani finished high school and at the time could not go to college because he was Hungarian. Hungarians were banned from higher education. This was my first education with prejudice, but he was able to secure a job with the city hall of the town.

In 1932, at the age of 5, my little friend Jozsi moved. I was enrolled in kindergarten as a 5-year-old. Kindergarten started at age 6, so I was an unofficial student. One day I was bored and took my lunch and started to head out the door of the school. The teacher said, "Where are you going?" I replied, "I am going home." "Why?", the teacher asked. I replied, "I am bored." The teacher let me go because I was underage anyway. Then a wonderful thing happened, a new neighbor moved into Jozsi's house, a little girl, Karla, who was Hungarian, and we became best friends. She spoke Hungarian and I learned Hungarian so we could communicate because I only spoke German in our house which was my father's wish.

In 1934, my father was transferred to another station. This was during the time when Yugoslavia's King Alexander I was assassinated by a Bulgarian, Vlado Chernozemski, who received weapons training in Hungary and put all Hungarians and Germans in danger of reprisal. So, we moved to Dragutinavo, a bigger station, and again my father operated the telegraph, acted as a ticket agent and utilized his technical skills when needed. We moved into the village next to a Yugoslavian family, a large family, who became dear friends of ours. My brother Nandi went to high school there. The winters were incredibly beautiful.

There was sledding, as part of fun times with our neighbors, who liked me and asked me to play and sled with them.

This is where my sister, Nuci, met Janos Vass and their courtship began, which led to their marriage. Nandi became a butcher by trade and started to work with a friend of my father, who was a butcher and owned a restaurant.

We stayed in the village for one year, and Father asked the railroad chief, who was a friend dating back to when they both entered the railroad industry together, for a favor to transfer him to a smaller station. The chief had good connections, so he was successful in transferring my father to Szanad, in Yugoslavia. I started a German school, which to my surprise was on the borders of Yugoslavia. I was not happy since I came from a Yugoslavian school and did not know the German alphabet. I struggled with my homework assignments which resulted in assistance from my father. He ended up going to the school, and he talked to my teacher and explained that my training in first grade was Yugoslavian language, not German language, and to switch me to a Yugoslavian school. The teacher, who liked me, wanted to teach me, and pledged to catch me up. My father received a first-grade book and helped me for one hour a day. In one month's time, I caught up with the entire class in the German school. An interesting point, there was a Yugoslavian school just one block away from our house and due to discrimination, Hungarians and Germans were not allowed to attend. The hate and prejudice extended into physical attacks that occurred after school by the Yugoslavian school's students. The bigger German kids could run away, but we smaller kids took a thrashing! So, it was reported to both schools. Again, I experienced discrimination and hate at this young age.

I attended German school up to fifth grade. Then we moved to Croatia because my father was transferred again. I attended a Croatian high school called Jupanya. I took the train from Gradiste to school. I remember a school dance when students, that were Yugoslavian, crashed the German party and attacked the students until everyone ran away.

Chapter 2
Borgond

In 1941, the Germans occupied Yugoslavia and my father again requested help. This time, it was from the Hungarian Embassy to move to Hungary. In October 1941, we moved to Hungary and took up residence at Borgond Train Station, a small station in the suburb of Szekesfehervar. We were housed in an apartment upstairs in the train station across from a military airport. I could see the airplanes taking off which was amazing to watch outside of our living room window. I did not know at that time that I would meet my future husband at this train station.

I was enrolled into a Hungarian high school. I had to learn the formal Hungarian language quickly. I was supposed to be in the second year of high school, and it was recommended that a private teacher help me with instruction to complete my high school education. So, I learned by listening to Hungarian radio. I read books to learn all of the intricacies of the Hungarian language and my mother helped me with the language

Borgond Train Station, home photo

which was her native tongue. I was ashamed because of the language barrier. I spoke broken Hungarian and continually worked on speech and dialect. I befriended a neighbor girl, Katalin, who was two years older, and she helped me with the language. She became a life-long, good friend.

I received an opportunity to work with my father, Matyas Menrath, at Borgond Station at the young age of 15, which required parental signature. Father was a seasoned professional who knew every aspect of rail and terminal function. He was the go-to person when a problem arose at any depot. He was called upon to correct the problems and get the train depots back to normal. His job description was known as the Corrective Action Professional.

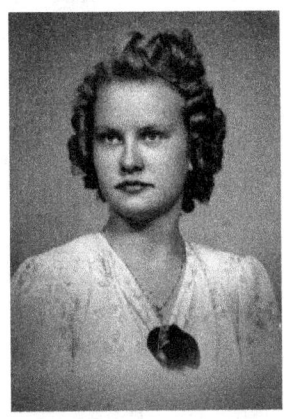

Iren's engagement photo.

In May of 1942, I was appointed to a Post Office training position and was tutored by Janos Vass, in Szekesfehervar, to handle the duties of Postal Service responsibilities. I worked in the Train Depot Post Office and received in-depth training on every facet of Post Office duty. I had gained the respect of my fellow employees and management at the station. After training, I was assigned the Post Office Manager position at Borgond Train Station. The staff gave me a going away party at my training station which was very special to me, and their kind words built confidence for my new position.

My responsibilities at Borgond were retrieving the mail bags from the caboose of every train that came through the terminal, sorting the mail, and placing the mail in the reserved Post Office boxes. I sold stamps, envelopes, money orders, and I prepared packages for shipment for residents shipping items out of town. Also, I was responsible for ordering supplies including depot supplies such as train tickets, schedules and money order forms. I had to do inventory and do the monthly closings. This was all made possible through my father's parental signature.

Upon my start at Borgond Station with my father in June 1942, I made friends with a seamstress named, Eszti. My friend Eszti was in her mid-twenties. She was attractive, flirtatious, and she was not shy to start conversations with soldiers from the adjacent air base next to Borgond. Eszti would invite me to go with her to Szekesfehervar to shop for fabrics. We would take the train into Szekesfehervar and shop for material fabrics to make dresses. She made the dresses, and I helped with the decisions on what colors and styles to create. I would get Western magazines and American magazines from my father in order to give them to Eszti so she could design the dresses from the magazines. My favorite dresses were the ones worn by Hollywood actresses from California, such as Katherine Hepburn, Bette Davis, and Joan Crawford, with my favorite being Olivia de Havilland. Her dresses were very attractive and stylish. Eszti made some wonderful duplicates of them. I believe wearing those dresses was how I was noticed by my future husband Lajos Suhajda, an Army Air-Corps Sergeant. I enjoyed my job, friends and family, and like my father, I too grew up quickly.

On one trip to Szekesfehervar, Eszti was in the train station restaurant/ tavern, and I was to meet her there at noon to shop for fabric. I had just picked up the mailbag from an inbound train and was sorting the mail when my father, Matyas Menrath, came into the office in a joyful mood and said in German, "Good morning to my lovely daughter. You didn't think your father would forget to get you the new edition of Life Magazine from my friends, did you? You do know family comes first, and I always take care of my loved ones."

I smiled and happily replied, "Good morning, Papa, we don't have to talk in German because we are not at home. I know your rule is German at home and Hungarian away from home. I know you left early this morning to get this for me, so thank you for the magazine. (as I smiled) I love the dresses and styles from America. Is Olivia de

Havilland in it? Your railroad friends are so kind to get this for me every month. Eszti and I are going to Szekesfehervar with the noon train to pick up fabric for the dress I am selecting."

He replied in Hungarian, "Yes, they are good people, I don't know if Olivia is in the magazine, and I am sure you will enjoy your shopping today. I left early to inspect the rail in Szekesfehervar Train Station. All is good. By the way, I saw Mr. Szarvas walking around the station and if he begs for food, do not give him any. We do not give out free handouts." I smiled and gave him a kiss on the cheek then said, "Yes, Papa, no free handouts." He added, "Good, I am headed out again to check the rail north of our station. See you tonight." He went out the back door.

I started to sort the mail from the mailbag and place it in the mail slots behind my desk for the villagers. The villagers would come in to pick up mail and buy stamps. I was getting a little warm, so I walked to the front door, which was a two-part door, a top part that opened and a bottom part. I opened the top of the door, and standing in front of the door was Mr. Szarvas. He was an older man in his fifties. His head was bowed down and as he peeked up at me, he said, "Good morning, Miss Iren, would you have any food that you could spare? I didn't eat breakfast and it is close to lunchtime. Is there anything, I can do to help out?"

I thought for a moment and developed a plan. I said, "Good morning, Mr. Szarvas. Actually, there is something you can do. I have to finish my office work and then go to Szekesfehervar at noon. I need the pigs fed at the end of the spur. Would you do that for me, and I'll have a lunch bag for you. The feed is in the wood box next to the pen." Mr. Szarvas cheered up and said, "Yes, I will be happy to do that. Thank you, Miss Iren." He walked off with a sense of purpose down the sidewalk and I went back to my filing saying to myself, "Yes, Papa, no free handouts." I smiled.

I finished my mail sorting at 11:45 a.m. and saw Mr. Szarvas at the front door. I said to him, "Did you finish feeding the pigs?" "Yes, Miss Iren, I did," replied Mr. Szarvas. I picked up my lunch bag, walked to the door and exclaimed, "Here is your lunch!" He replied, "But this is your lunch, Miss Iren. I can't take your lunch!" "I am grateful for your help. I will be fine. Enjoy your lunch." I stated this as I patted his hand that was on top of the half door. He thanked me again and walked away. I saw the clock was 11:55 a.m. and I quickly locked up the office then ran next door to the restaurant.

I walked into the restaurant and noticed Eszti sitting at the bar. I walked up to her and said, "Hi! Eszti, are you ready to go to the train? It's just pulling in." She said, "Yes, let's go!" (with a mischievous gleam in her eyes) She stated, "Do you see those two soldiers in the back? They are good looking, aren't they?" I looked back and noticed two Army Air Corp officers looking at us and I replied, "We don't have time to visit. We have to go." We left and went to the train. As we got on board and sat down, I noticed to my surprise that they followed us and proceeded to sit down next to us. I was told by my parents not to talk to soldiers.

Lajos and friend Sergeant Darvasi, home photo.

One soldier boldly introduced their names to both of us. "Hello, my name is Sergeant Lajos Suhajda, and this is Sergeant Imre Darvasi. We are pilots at Borgond Army Air Base in the advanced flight training program with the ME109 Messerschmitt aircraft. What are your names?" I heard Eszti introduce herself, "Hello, my name is Eszti, I am a seamstress. Iren and I are going into town to shop for spools of materials for new dresses." I continued to look out the window at the beautiful forest scenery and ignored them. Suddenly, I felt a tap on my shoulder and Lajos was introducing himself again and asked what my name was. Feeling awkward I mumbled, "Iren", which he didn't understand and asked again, so I slowly said, "Iren, (EERANE)!"

Eszti interrupted us and clarified, "This is Iren Menrath. She works at Borgond Train Station as the Post Office Manager." I looked at Eszti with a why did you say that look and turned to look out the window. Meanwhile Lajos talked about his advance training with the ME-109 and reported that in September he would be finished and receive his combat orders. The whole time he spoke, I continued to look out the window. Eszti jumped in again and added, "Iren is a very responsible young lady." Eszti talked about her seamstress projects and how we were going to Szekesfehervar to pick up dress making materials. Lajos admired my appearance, but when we arrived at Szekesfehervar, we ended up parting ways, and both of us went shopping for the materials we needed. I looked at Eszti and said, "Why did you tell them all of that? I am not interested in soldiers. Sometimes you are impossible." I found out later that when we parted, Lajos told his friend, "I will marry that girl one day."

Lajos found out that I lived on the top floor in the apartment with my parents at the railroad station. He kept hanging around to see me. I tried to avoid him, as long as I could. He came in to buy stamps and mail letters to his parents, so I eventually talked to him. Lajos asked me if I could go for a walk or just sit and talk. I continually replied, "I am very busy with my duties and do not have time. Perhaps another time." He was very persistent and came around on a regular basis trying to establish a relationship. Finally, he started to "get the picture" and reduced his visits, which caught my attention. The real truth was that I started getting fond of him.

One Saturday morning, I was out feeding the chickens and livestock behind the Post Office building, which was the location of our garden, bomb shelter, and animal cages filled with pigs, chickens, and ducks. Lajos was walking by, and I nodded to him. Just then he came over to talk and said, "Hello, is this one of your other duties?" "Yes, it is," I replied and continued, "Hello Lajos, I am sorry I have been avoiding you, but the truth is that my parents do not want me to befriend military personnel. You see, they don't trust soldiers. They believe you are opportunists and lack responsibility. You move from place to place, and it's not good to establish relationships. I do have time for a walk this afternoon if you wish?" Lajos smiled and replied, "I understand. I would be honored to escort you for a walk. What time can I come by?" I looked at him and said, "It will be better if we meet at the South Depot entrance and walk from there. Let's say in an hour."

I changed my clothes, brushed my hair quickly and went to the entrance which was adjacent to a mountain range trail. Lajos was waiting there for me. We walked and he talked about his flying experience. It all intrigued me. He told me about his training with the Italian training bi-plane made by Bucher Flugzeubau Biplane Company, which was half wood and half metal. A fellow pilot ahead of him on the final test flight day did his maneuvers, takeoff, landing, target

Lajos Suhajda, Student pilot, used this plane

Role   Basic trainer
Manufacturer   Bücker Flugzeugbau
Designer   Carl Bücker
First flight   27 April 1934
Introduction   1935 (Luftwaffe)

shooting, steep climb into a stall, and then he went into a spin. He was to correct out of the spin by turning into the spin to level out and pulling back to climb out to normal flight. He did everything, but in the spin, he could not correct his position and ended up crashing, killing himself instantly. Lajos's test was rescheduled for the next day. Lajos explained the event, "Everyone was there. My parents and my brothers. My older brother, Joseph, was already a pilot, so I was determined to give them a good show and to graduate. It was my turn, and I repeated the maneuvers, climbed to a stall position, and I went into the spin. I followed the process to correct the spin, but I could not straighten the aircraft. I kept trying and realized it was not working. The ground was coming up fast, but I was at an acceptable height, so I accelerated with more power and tried the correction again. It was working! As I disappeared behind the tree line at the airfield, everyone was beside themselves, and they were thinking, "Not another plane crash?" My brothers were yelling to pull up! While everyone was expecting to hear a crash, I skimmed the weeds on the adjacent field behind the tree line. Then I pulled up and soared back up to a straight and level flight. I landed and was met by my Superior Officer, and I was debriefed on the stall. It was discovered that the wood and metal design on the aircraft caused a failure in the spin maneuver, and if I had not increased the speed, I also would have crashed, and you would not be talking to me today. I did receive a special accommodation and advancement to the top-level pilot training for the ME109, and here I am."

Lajos looked at me and said, "Tell me about your family." I told him about living in Yugoslavia and a story about my father. "We were transferred to Szanad, where my father was highly respected as a railroad man. He was an excellent trouble shooter and was in high demand. One day a local farmer came into the terminal and asked for my father, Matyas Menrath, and reported that he had a large grain order that had to be shipped out to Italy. He wanted it to be packaged in 25 kilo bags and loaded onto rail cars. My father apologized and explained that the railroad did not offer that type of service. The shipments had to be ready to load upon arrival at the train station. The farmer asked my father, if he paid him an agreeable sum, would he consider doing the job after hours?" My father paused, considered the offer and agreed to 75,000 forint per week for one month's work.[1] It was a tough job, and he worked 7 hours a night after normal hours, a total of 15 hours per day, to convert bulk grain into bags and load them into box cars for delivery. He kept it a secret but was discovered when the farmer stopped by, as my father was out on a project. He bragged to my father's Supervisor, Mr. Weiss, about the outstanding job he was doing for him. Well, his Supervisor, Mr. Weiss, a Jewish man, was jealous that my father had this opportunity. Then he fired him and took over the farmer's job opportunity. That is when Father became a fan of Hitler, because Hitler accused the Jews of everything that was wrong with Germany, and how they manipulated and cheated to gain superiority. After two weeks had gone by, the Railroad Executives were asking for my father's help with a list of problems. Mr. Weiss had lied and said my father had quit. A top official, Mr. Toth, came by to talk to my father about quitting. Father was angry and told him everything about how he did not quit, but that Mr. Weiss had fired him. Mr. Toth was stunned at the dishonesty and said he would be reinstated and receive back pay for his time lost. Mr. Weiss was fired for his unprofessional actions. My father was a proud and determined man with a good heart, "just in case you meet him."

Lajos asked to meet me again and I said, "Yes!" We met up several times in secret. He told me about his ambitions after the war. He wanted to be an airline pilot. Our walks were informative, a form of introduction, instead of romantic interludes. It was a way of learning

---

[1] Hungarian currency on economic market.

about each other and peeking behind the curtain. After a few walks, I experienced my first kiss. I was hesitant at first but enjoyed it. The later walks were without resistance and were more passionate. Lajos asked to meet my parents, and I always told him 'later'. I kept the secret of my age a "hush, hush" since Lajos was 9 years older than me.

Our neighbor, my friend Katalin's mother, saw us a few times and came up to my mother and told her, "Anna, a soldier is courting your daughter. I have seen them on walks together." When my mother found out she was upset and questioned me, "I was told by Mrs. Kalman that you have had rendezvous with a soldier? Is that true? You have been telling me that you were going out at night with your friends, Lynusos or Magda, and now it turns out you are meeting a soldier?" I lowered my head and said, "Yes." She continued, "You are a child of 15 and not at an age to date, especially not soldiers. I have told you how soldiers behave, and they are not reliable and not trustworthy. I want to meet him and talk to him. You tell him your mother and father wish to meet him." My father was terribly upset when he found out about my secret rendezvous and gave me a lecture as well. I was daddy's girl, and he agreed to meet Lajos.

It was a sunny Sunday afternoon when Lajos came over to the train depot, and walked up the back stairs to our apartment and knocked on the door. My mother answered the door and introduced herself, "Good afternoon, I am Anna Menrath, Iren's mother, please come in." My father got up from his kitchen chair and walked over, hand raised, and introduced himself, "I am Matyas Menrath, Iren's father." He shook hands and continued, "I understand that you wish to date my daughter, and truth be told, I am against it because she is too young. Fifteen is not an acceptable dating age. So, please sit down." They sat at the kitchen table, as did all of us, and Father asked the key question, "What are your intentions?" Lajos replied, "I have a deep affection for Iren and wish to spend time with her to see if our interests are shared."

"I am glad you did not say marriage," replied Father. "If you had said that our meeting would have been over." Then he paused and continued, "I do have a timeline that I will present to you, and it is a form of chaperone dating up to her 17th birthday. After that we will have a celebration announcing her engagement. I will not allow any marriage before Iren's 18th birthday. What do you think of this timeline?" Lajos, surprised, replied, "I like your timeline and believe it will be best for all of us. I appreciate your confidence in me, and I won't let you down." My father said, "Very good, now tell me about your pilot training at the base." Then he poured a glass of red wine for his guest. Lajos began, "I am a Sergeant in the Hungarian Army Air Corps, and I am in Advanced Pilot Training for the ME109, Messerschmitt Aircraft. I will finish October 1943. After the war, my plan is to join the airline industry as a pilot."

As mother and I set the table for a Hungarian porkolt dinner, Lajos and father continued to talk about the war and who was winning. Father explained, "I was a fan of Adolf Hitler until I discovered the Polish atrocities of 1939 and how they were all true. I learned about them through trusted railroad friends, a form of communication we shared when I traveled from station to station to troubleshoot rail problems. I received reports about the Polish atrocities where villagers were murdered, and the Polish resistance was making efforts to fight the Nazis. I didn't believe it. I wore a half mustache like Hitler until I saw photos of the dead villagers lined in rows. A conductor friend of mine showed me these pictures. I bought into the Jewish hatred because of some unscrupulous Jewish men that cheated me out of a business opportunity. Seeing

women and children murdered by these butchers made me shave the mustache off. That is our secret."

Chapter 3
Jewish Deportation Borgond

I had some very dramatic moments at Borgond when the Germans were deporting Italian and Hungarian Jews to the death camps. At that time, I did not know where the trains were headed and for what reason. I pressed for answers!

Jewish deportation train, June 1, 1943, Wikipedia

It was a hot day on June 1, 1943, as a train pulled into the station, and I left the office to retrieve the mailbag from the caboose. As I was walking towards the caboose, I noticed all the people looking at the train. I noticed the bars in the corners of the rail cars. I thought they were cattle cars, and I heard muffled sounds. I continued walking and noticed a door slightly open about twelve inches, and I saw a little Italian girl, no more than ten years old with the saddest and most frightened look on her face. I stopped in horror, realizing that this train was a Jewish deportation train. Not knowing what to do, but I wanted to do something, I yelled out to the people on the platform, "Does anyone have any food?" An elderly lady who was going to visit her son at the neighboring airbase replied, "I have apples!" She walked over and gave me an apple, and I gave it to the little girl. The horror that followed made all of us cry. As I gave her the apple, we saw what seemed to be

50 arms circled around the little girl with hands open for an apple. We were devastated by this scene. Many of the bystanders had their hands to their mouths with tears welling up in their eyes. Just at that moment, a German soldier ran toward us taking his machine gun from his shoulder and yelling, "Halt! Halt!" He continued in German while pointing his machine gun, "What are you doing?" I answered him in perfect German, which surprised him, "What are you doing with these people?" He lowered his tone seeing that it was a pretty German fraulein talking to him and replied, "These are not people. They are Jews. They are going to work in labor camps." I snapped back, "They are starving and need food and water!" He replied, "They will be fed at the next station." I interrupted him and said, "Do you see the pig pen at the end of the spur?" I pointed to the pen. He answered, "Yes." I continued, "We treat our pigs better than you treat these human beings!" He was flustered and noticed the elderly lady crying and yelled out, "What are you crying about? Do you know I can throw you on this train too?" The train whistle blew, and he ran back to his post. I also ran to the caboose and picked up the mailbag. On my walk back to the office I cried. As I sat in my chair with tears in my eyes, a man dressed in a suit came in and introduced himself, "Hello, I am Raoul Wallenberg, Swedish Diplomat. Has the deportation train come

Iren Menrath Post Office Manager 1943, Borgond Train Station

through yet?[2]" I replied, "Yes, it has. It left 5 minutes ago. I am Iren Menrath, Post Office Manager." When Raoul saw that I was upset he asked, "Miss Menrath, why are you crying?" I explained the incident to him and stated, "I felt so helpless! I wanted to do something for those suffering people." He compassionately replied, "You are a special, courageous, young lady. You did all you could. You are to be commended. I will leave you with this thought. There are two types of people in this world, human beings and others who do not care about human life. God bless you and good day, Miss Menrath." He turned and left.

One week later on another hot summer afternoon, another Jewish deportation train came through the station. As I started to walk to pick up the mailbags, I saw Mr. Szarvas. I asked him to spray water in the barred windows of the train so the people could refresh themselves. On my way back from the caboose, I saw a German soldier get off the train from the passenger compartment, and he spotted Mr. Szarvas spraying the water. He started to run toward him, pulling his machine gun off his shoulder. Witnessing that, I ran to intercept his path placing myself, in between the German soldier and Mr. Szarvas. The German soldier, an older man, yelled, "Halt! Halt! What are you doing?" Mr. Szarvas dropped his hose. I replied in German to the soldier, "I told him to spray water in the barred windows of the train so the people can get some water. They were hitting their metal cups on the bars." The German soldier was surprised by my boldness and replied, "These are Jews going to work camps. We control their food and water. You're not allowed any contact with them!" He turned and walked back to the passenger car as the train whistle blew.

---

[2] Raoul Wallenberg, Swedish Diplomat led one of the most extensive and successful Jewish rescue efforts during the era of WWII.

Lajos in his Army Air Corp bi-wing training flight, Home Photo

Lajos finished his classroom training that same day, June 8th, 1943, and he celebrated with a few drinks. I came out of the office and saw him coming out of the restaurant/ bar. I could see that he was tipsy. He had a postcard in his hand announcing his classroom graduation after he passed his final flight test. I escorted him to the mailbox. It was a dark overcast evening, and I helped him maneuver over the 6 railroad tracks toward his base. He leaned on me a few times to catch his balance. I watched him carefully to make sure that he got back to his base. As we parted, he called out, "Iren!" I answered him, "What?" He started to come back my way. I said, "Don't come back, you need to go to your base and go to sleep." He replied, "That's right, OK." He turned and kept walking. As I watched him, I could hear him repeating my name over and over again until he disappeared into the night. Then I went back to my office.

The postcard that Lajos wrote at the train station, while he was intoxicated, was to be for his parents. Instead, he wrote the address to himself. He received the postcard days later and was totally surprised! Later on, we had a good laugh about the whole thing.

Iren and Lajos Anniversary picture.

On Sunday, June 13, 1943, we were engaged. A week later my father decided to announce our engagement with a party. All were invited! Family, friends, and guests. All were present except my older brother, Jani and his wife. I was missing my older brother Jani, who I would later find out was murdered by Yugoslavian vigilantes. It was a warm sunny day, and all had a great time. Father met Lajos's Commanding Officer, Captain Rudi Rothenfelder, who announced that he was assigning Lajos to the advanced ME-109 instrument training. This instrument rating instruction lasted until October 1943. Upon graduation, he would be assigned to the Eastern Front to fight the Russians. Father took this opportunity to invite Captain Rudi Rothenfelder to dinner the following Saturday, June 20th. Captain Rothenfelder accepted and stated, "I will be there sharply at 7:00 p.m." He was fond of Lajos and believed he was his top pilot in his ME-109 training squadron.

Captain Rothenfelder 1940 Photo

Saturday came, and as day turned into night the stars filled the evening sky when he arrived with Lajos in a staff car. He greeted all of us with kindness and requested to be called Rudi. My father, speaking German, asked him how the war was going, and much to our surprise his reply was that things were not going well. His belief was that Germany was losing the war, and he felt genuinely concerned for his men that he was sending off to the Eastern Front. That is when he explained a plan to promote Lajos to advance night flight instruction. Rudi talked about his family and hoped the war would not hurt the innocent people on both sides. I was impressed by this compassionate man. We listened carefully as he told a story of a dog fight between his plane. the ME-109 and an American P-51 aircraft over the Ionian Sea of Greece. "It was a heated battle! We were both maneuvering for position, taking shots on our maneuvers, but missing. We did dives and rolls with steep banks to a climb to try to position into a rear kill position. We both banked in opposite directions, rolled, and climbed only to end up, face-to-face. We both fired, and we shot each other down. I bailed out, and so did the American. We landed our parachutes 50 meters apart from each other in the sea. I pulled my raft from my backpack and blew it up. I had an injured leg because a bullet had grazed my thigh. I pulled myself into my raft as I was watching the American. He was having difficulty blowing up his raft. He had a shoulder injury from a bullet going through his shoulder into his backpack, and it punctured his raft. I paddled over to him, as quickly as possible, because he was barely hanging on. Reaching out my hand, the American grabbed hold of it. I pulled him into my raft, and there we were looking at each other. I knew a little English, so I said "Hello" to him, and I asked him where he was shot. He replied, 'My left shoulder.' He asked me where I was shot, and I told him that it was my right thigh. Four hours later, we were picked up by a Greek merchant ship. We were dispatched to the same hospital and became good friends. I learned his name was Lieutenant Bradley Adams. The hospital contacted the Red Cross, and because Bradley was an American, the hospital that we were in received all its' medical supplies for all the patients. Even though our fight was in the air, our compassion for human life brought us together, not as enemies, but as friends." I knew from his story what a good man Rudi was.

As Rudi was leaving, I approached him to ask if there was anything he could do to not send Lajos to the Eastern Front which was certain death. He looked at me with a stern look and asked, "Do you know what you are saying?" He said no more and got into his jeep. Then Lajos came out, got into the jeep, and they drove away.

Captain Rothenfelder's Hungarian Army Air Corp squadron 1943 Captain Rothenfelder is standing, Lajos Suhajda is in the second row number 11.
ME109 in background   1943

The training was finishing up, and Lajos's last requirement for testing was target shooting. The plane had accumulated many hours of wear and tear on its mechanical parts from all the pilot training. Lajos told me to watch his final take-off test from the upstairs living room window that overlooked the airport runway. He would flutter his wings up and down at takeoff, so my mother and I would know it was he. We watched one takeoff after another takeoff, but there was no signal. I walked away from the window for a moment, and my mother watched the next pilot climb into the cockpit and start his take-off. He was rolling down the runway picking up speed, and all of a sudden, the left front wheel came off. The plane cartwheeled and landed upside down with the wheels up. I was sitting down in the living room after all the waiting when I heard Mother scream out, "Oh my God, whoever was in that airplane is dead!" The emergency vehicles were speeding to the scene.

Plane crashed upside down, Wikipedia

As the emergency team arrived with fellow pilots, they noticed the plane was leaking fuel. The crew was banging on the fuselage when Lajos yelled, "Stop! There is fuel pouring out of the aircraft, and one spark will set it on fire!" Lajos's life was saved because a smaller pilot flew before him, and when he got into the cockpit, the harness was smaller and tighter when he was strapped in. The crew's teammate told him that he should adjust the harness to fit him better, but Lajos said it was all right. That action saved his life.

While Lajos was being pulled out of the wreckage, I was running across the railroad tracks onto the field to the fence where two security guards approached me and asked what I was doing. I explained, "I saw the accident from our window, pointing to the train station at the open window. I believe the pilot is my fiancé!" The guard asked, "What makes you think he is your fiancé?" "He told me that when he takes off, he would shimmy his wings to let me know it was him. I just have a feeling this was him. He is the last flyer, and no shimmying has taken place." The guard asked, "What is his name?" "Sergeant Lajos

Suhajda," I replied. They looked at each other, paused, and then replied, "No, it was not him." I asked, "Is he with the other pilots at the base, and can I talk to him now?" "No, you cannot," they responded again. A little frustrated, I asked, "Can I talk to his Superior Officer, Captain Rothenfelder?" "No, you will have to go to the front gate and enter there and request a meeting," replied the guard. Then they firmly reported, "Civilians are not allowed to approach the airfield. This is a time of war and security, and it is a top priority. There are spies that could collect information. We understand that you are not a spy, but please follow our instructions."

I knew from their answers that it was Lajos on the plane. I returned home to change my shoes because they were muddy from running to the airfield. I then took the bus to the main gate of the air base. Upon my arrival, I reported to the duty officer that I had witnessed an accident on the runway and suspected that it was my fiancé, and I wanted to talk with Sergeant Lajos Suhajda. The duty officer said, "I will send a soldier to the airfield to report to Sergeant Suhajda that he has a visitor." I replied, "I talked with two security guards at the airfield who reported he was not there and told me to come here and ask for him."

Sergeant Darvasi, Lajos's friend.

The duty officer sent the soldier anyway. Sergeant Darvasi, a friend of Lajos and me, came out of the infirmary, which was the next building over. He noticed me and immediately said, "Hello Iren! It is good to see you. Don't worry about anything. Lajos is alright with no serious injuries. The left wheel came off during takeoff, and the plane crashed. Since he was strapped in very tightly, it prevented serious injury." Sergeant Darvasi excused himself and went over to the duty officer to confirm who I was, and then he got a pass for me to visit Lajos in the infirmary. [3]

Sergeant Darvasi got my clearance pass, and we went into the infirmary. Sergeant Darvasi asked me to wait outside of the entrance to the patient ward. He went in and told everyone that a female visitor was about to enter and that all should cover accordingly. He then came out and invited me to come in. All the patients had a linen wall divider separating them from other patients. I was concerned as I walked in, thinking that perhaps Sergeant Darvasi asked Lajos to cover himself up to cover any broken bones from the accident which would make me nervous and afraid of what I would see. As I greeted him and kissed him, I asked him how he was. He repeated what Sergeant Darvasi had reported to me. Lajos was pale from the shock of the accident, but there were no broken bones. Relieved, I told him, "God was watching over you, and it was a miracle that you were not hurt." He smiled and said, "Well, my guardian angel was watching over me from her window at the train station." That made me laugh as I blushed at his compliment.

After this test flight, Lajos was to be transferred to the Eastern Front to fight the Russian troops. He did not complete his firing range flight, so he had to wait until his test was completed. I remembered a month before the accident at the dinner with Captain Rothenfelder and wondered if this accident may change Lajos's future assignment. I do not know if my question about changing his orders entered his mind, but it seems he had a way to execute the order due to the accident.

In October 1943, Lajos was ordered to go to Szeget for his advanced night training instruction that lasted through the summer of 1944.

---

[3] Infirmary is a military institution providing care for the injured and Illnesses'.

Lajos became an instructor pilot at a training airport at Kenjeri, which lasted until November of 1944.

The war was taking its toll, and Borgond Train Station was a target by both American and Russian aircraft to bomb the tracks to cut supply lines. One morning I was in the back of the building feeding the chickens when I watched the chickens line up and walk back into their chicken coup. I had never seen that before during the daytime, and I wondered what was happening. Two hours later, Borgond received an air attack. There were villagers in the train station office as the sirens sounded. I shouted, "Take shelter! There is an air raid." A lady asked, "Can I please get a book of stamps?" I anxiously replied, "We need to take shelter!" She kept pleading, and I realized that it would be faster to sell her the book of stamps than to argue. I sold her the stamps and quickly went to the back door. As I looked out, I saw a Russian plane flying over and shooting at the tracks, and I heard the ricochet of the bullets. The Russians also shot at civilians on the railroad station grounds.

The bomb shelter behind the Borgond Train Station building that Iren dove into.

So, I waited until the plane passed and then ran out towards the bomb shelter which was thirty meters away. My father was yelling, "IREN! IREN! Run, hurry, run!" What I did not know was that another plane had turned from around my building, and it was behind me. I ran as fast as I could and dove into the shelter as my father slammed the iron door. The machine gun bullets hit the door in a rapid succession, and we heard the ricochets off the door which scared all of us. When I was in the bomb shelter, I told the story of the chickens, and we watched the chickens closely thereafter, securing a chicken air defense system that gave us advanced warnings of other attacks, allowing us to be ready in the future!

Chapter 4

End of WWII

On Tuesday, September 5, 1944, I visited my sister, Nuci, and my brother-in-law, Janos Vass, who was the Kenjeri Depot Manager. They asked me if I would consider transferring to the Kenjeri Post Office to be the Post Office Manager. The lady who previously held that position quit because of the escalation of the war. The job was offered to me, and I accepted. My father signed the acceptance papers for the Post Office Manager's position because I was seventeen years old, and I had to be eighteen years of age to officially sign. So, I had one week's training at Kenjeri, and I started on September 11, 1944. I managed the post office for the village. I was the only person who operated the train station's post office, collected the mail bags from the trains, was responsible for depot inventory plus purchases, sorted the mail into the villagers' post office boxes, sold stamps, processed money orders, and serviced the community with incoming and outgoing packages, just as I had done previously in Borgond. At Kenjeri, I received high evaluations and was asked to stay on after my marriage.

It was a Friday, November 10, 1944, and we received word of the evacuation of Borgond Train Station. The war was taking its toll on Germany, and the Germans were destroying all assets that could not be taken with them. We learned that Borgond was to be blown up. I knew Kenjeri would be next on their list. My short time with Lajos was ending, and I feared what the future would bring. So, we headed to the border city of Kenjeri, where Lajos was stationed. My father was reassigned to a nearby railroad station in a village called Szeldemulk.

The war changed all our plans, and in November 1944, the Russian advancement into Hungary was taking a different path, and the German squadrons were retreating. Lajos's duty was changed, and he was to be assigned to the Front Lines. He was transferred to a Support Airport Base for defensive purposes. The plans for our marriage were scheduled for April 2, 1945. I was preparing to buy a wedding dress and veil, but unfortunately, the Russian advancement changed our wedding plans. Lajos had a meeting with Captain Rothenfelder, and he reported that a strategic surrender to the US Troops was being planned. Only wives were allowed to travel with the convoy, but for me, he was making an exception. He directed Lajos to call the post office and leave word for me to be there at 1:00 pm for his call. He wanted us to marry right away, but unfortunately, my supervisor would not allow me to leave. He reported to come to the airfield, and we were to be married at the Kenjeri Air Base. This was one week before our scheduled April 2 wedding.

My parents had a major decision to make: To either let me elope or to face the Russian advancement, in which it was reported that young women were being raped, assaulted, and killed. My father had heard from his railroad colleagues that some parents were hiding their daughters from the Russians, and when they were found, many of these atrocities were committed. My father decided that it was time for intelligent decision-making, and he agreed to let me go to Lajos's base so we could marry.

My father instructed that I should meet up with a German convoy in the village of Szekesfehervar. I went to the village and met the German Officer in command. He heard my story and my request to meet up with my fiancé. He reported that he had received a communication from Captain Rudi Rothenfelder, and he agreed to allow me to travel with his squadron. So, my parents packed my clothes, some food for the trip, and pillows to use when sleeping. On March 26, 1945, at 3:00

pm, I said goodbye to my weeping mother and hugged my father to join the convoy. As we left, I cried in having to leave them. The fear of the unknown was unbearable to think about! Would I witness the victimization of civilians by the Russian Army? Would this be the last time I saw my parents? Would our convoys be in danger during our journey? The Allies would bomb convoys along the way. Both Russian and American planes would attack. So, our journey was very dangerous as well. The Kenjeri Base, which was on the way, was to join our convoy too. They were headed toward the Western Front into Germany to surrender to the Americans with us. The decision was based on the reputation and treatment by Americans as being better with prisoners of war than the Russians.

Lajos's squadron map racing to surrender to the allied American Army being chased by the Russian troops.

Captain Rothenfelder took charge of the convoy when the divisions joined up. His strategy was to travel at night knowing the convoys were being bombed. So, the race was on with the Russian Army chasing our convoy with a mission to kill the German soldiers, and our convoy was racing through Austria to Passau, Germany to surrender to the American Army.

Hungarian Army squadron race to surrender to USA Allied troops, March 1945, Wikipedia.

As we traveled, we saw the devastation of war, dead horses, overturned vehicles with dead civilians, German soldiers killed next to the road, and many wounded. We raced to Passau to The Pocking Airport, where the Russian troops were advancing and were right on our heels. We arrived on the west side of the Danube River, and the Russians arrived on the East side at about the same time. We won the race, and we then surrendered to the US Army. What a jubilation! We celebrated, cheered, and waved at the Russian troops. Captain Rothenfelder had ordered white flags to be placed on the trucks to show our commitment to the surrender, with hopes that any aircraft would spot the signal and not drop bombs on the convoy. Traveling at night was definitely a strategic move for all of us! The last two hours were nerve-racking because the Russians found out and wanted to catch our convoy. They shot mortars and flares to stop our advancement, but luckily, we were out of range. As we listened to the mortar attacks, it gave us a sense of how close the mortars were to our convoy. That was motivation enough to move as fast as we could. The journey to reach the USA territory took approximately 13 hours. Our convoy was totally exhausted, but so very happy that it was all over!

Our convoy was met by American soldiers, and it was a very peaceful surrender. The white flags had worked, and we became Prisoners of War. We were escorted to the Pocking Air Base in Bavaria which became our Prisoner of War Camp. The Army had accommodations ready for us there. This was where we were held and processed from April to October 1945. During this time, as the war raged on, we were given an opportunity for Lajos to ask Captain Rothenfelder if we could be married at Pocking. He said that he would seek permission from the American Commander, with no promises, but that he would ask. The Commander of the base agreed, and we were married in a school adjacent to the town church. We were not residents of the city. Therefore, we could not get permission to marry in the church. Captain Rothenfelder was Lajos's best man. We were married on April 21, 1945, eight days before my eighteenth birthday. The wedding ceremony was short but beautiful. On May 8, 1945, a joyous announcement came that the war was over! Lajos and I were ecstatic with happiness that we could now create new plans for our lives. We met with counselors who presented options for our consideration, and one of the options was to settle in the United States. Sergeant Bradford, US Army, debriefed Lajos and me on the options to refugee to the United States, and he provided a strong argument for our freedom and opportunities. At that time, our hearts were with family in Hungary, and we chose to return home to Hungary. It was our belief that Hungary was to be free, and we did not know at the time what Russian plans awaited us.

Many people, after the declared end of WWII, wanted to leave and walk back to Hungary, which was not advised. Lajos, being impatient, wanted to return as soon as possible, but I convinced him that mass transit was the best way to travel. I told him that we should wait until the trains were commissioned to transport us to Hungary, which occurred in October 1945. It was ironic that we returned in the box cars that about a thousand Jewish people were transported in to the concentration camps. They were transported to their deaths, and we were transported to a new life. A very sad situation in the circle of life.

I was worried about my parents and family, not knowing what happened to us after we left. I did not have any communication with them. I tried not to think negative thoughts, and I just looked forward to returning home! On our return, we took the train into Sopron, Hungary, and we pulled into the station. We waited for a passenger train from Kenyeri to pull in before us. Later, I discovered that my mother, Anna, was on that train, and she saw our box car train which she believed was a train returning Hungarian soldiers to Hungary. She departed her train and walked towards our train, yelling to the people she saw, "Where are you coming from?" The reply was, "This is the Prisoner of War train returning from Germany." She yelled again and asked, "Do you know a Sergeant Suhajda?" One of the soldiers in the group answered back, "Yes, he is on this train!" My mother was so happy that she broke down and cried at the news. She had not known if we had been killed in the war, so the news became overwhelming. She collected herself and again asked, "Where is the train headed?" "The train is headed to Kaposvar," he replied. Kaposvar was the indoctrination debrief center where the soldiers were processed and questioned. The debriefers asked questions like, "Why did you join the military? Why did you go to Germany?" Lajos answered those questions simply and directly, "These were our commanding officer's orders. A refusal of orders in a war is subject to a firing squad."

After the interrogation at Kaposvar, we were free to go. The city of Kaposvar is close to Godisa where my brother-in-law, Janos Vass, was the Chief of the Railroad Station. So, we decided to go to see my sister, Nuci. To my surprise, my father, Matyas Menrath, arrived the next day. My mother reported the news to him, and he knew that after the debrief, we would go to Janos and Nuci's house. My father was so jubilant and explained the devastating news of the war, which led us to believe that he may have been killed.

Katalina Komaromi Menrath, Jani's wife, 1943 home photo.

My father received a letter from my brother Jani's wife, Katalin Komaromi Menrath, that Jani was killed in Gombos, Yugoslavia. That increased our family's sorrow. On June 9, 1945, a Saturday evening, they were having dinner at Katalin's parents' house, when the front door was kicked in, and a group of partisans entered the dining room with weapons drawn. The leader announced, "By the order of Tito, the Communist Prime Minister of Yugoslavia, all Hungarians, Germans, and sympathizers are to be arrested. Get up and come with us!" They took Mr. Komaromi and Janos. These partisans had secured a citizen list from the Village City Hall, and any German or Hungarian name was targeted for assassination.

Janos Menrath, murdered by Yugoslavian vigilantes, 1945. Home Photo.

They marched them off into the night with shovels in their hands. They made them dig their own graves, shot them and buried them. We suspect that they took them into the nearby woods. We searched for months to find them, in order to give them a religious burial, but we never did find their graves.

I cried for days…I could not believe how hate drives people to kill innocent human beings because of a name that reflects a certain nationality or government. This was Tito's way of getting even and allowing criminals in the name of Communism to kill innocent Germans and

Hungarians as a post-war gesture. It seems that evil had entered our daily lives, and the only people that could be trusted were family.

Chapter 5

Civilian Life

So, we stayed for a week with my parents and then decided to visit Lajos's mother and father in Dombegyhaz. Lajos had two brothers, Pista and his older brother, József. We found out that József, also an Army pilot, tragically died in a Russian Prisoner of War Camp. We learned that the Russians had threatened to take all the Hungarian soldiers to Siberia to a labor camp.[4] Pista had visited József at the Prisoner of War Camp. József told him, "I will not go to Siberia. Over my dead body will I go!" We had learned that he had eaten tobacco which caused kidney failure and thus had died by his own hand of nicotine poisoning. If József had waited one more week, he would have learned that the Prisoners of War were to be released. It was very sad. The news was devastating, and a cloud of sorrow hung over his parents' house. József was buried in Sopron.

Threshing machine that Lajos maintained for his father's business., Wikipedia.

---

[4] Siberian labor camp, also known as Gulag was a system of forced labor camps in the Soviet Union.

As Lajos searched for a new life for us, he sought employment with trusted family members.

Lajos's father, József Suhajda Sr., had a small business selling threshing machines to farmers and offered Lajos a job to repair machines when they broke down. The pay was not enough to support a family, so Lajos tried to secure his own position. The depressed economy made jobs hard to secure. My husband tried to rely on his flying expertise to secure a job, but that industry was very selective after the war. Unfortunately, since he was a Prisoner of War to the Americans, he was turned down for aviation positions and also blacklisted.[5]

In dire need to make income, Lajos agreed to work as a maintenance man on the threshing machines for his father. He also worked on wheat harvests as a second job using the threshing machines.[6]

Shortly after Lajos worked for his father, a dispute occurred with his brother Pista. The threshing machine business was owned and operated by his father and two brothers, Pista and József Jr.. When József Jr. died in the Prisoner of War Camp, Pista wanted a larger share of the revenues which would reduce the pay for Lajos. That salary reduction was not a fair option for Lajos, and he decided to leave the business. Unfortunately, these feelings became a family dispute for many years, and the

Pista Suhajda, Lajos's brother. Home photograph.

---

[5] Blacklisted is a list of people, that are shunned or excluded from a chosen profession or opportunity. Lajos was blacklisted in Hungary by the Russians.
[6] Threshing machine is a piece of farm equipment that separates grain seed from the stalks and husks. It does so by beating the plant to make the seeds fall out.

brothers would not speak to each other.

During our stay from October 1945 to September 1946, Lajos's father, Józef Sr., had died of diabetes. Lajos looked for a new job and went to Kis-Dombegyhaz, the neighboring town and secured a job as a machine operator. Manufacturing was booming at that time, and machinists were in high demand.

I became pregnant in 1946, and we moved into a very small house with one bedroom and a kitchen. We were very poor. As my due date approached, I wrote to my parents and reported our situation, and I asked them for help. My mother came in the first part of April 1947, with all the support needed, such as clothing, diapers, bottles, blankets, etc., which was a blessing, and we were so thankful. My son, Józef Suhajda, was born on May 1, 1947.

Lajos was proud to have a son. The belief was that a son would carry on the surname within the family. Józef, nicknamed Jozi, named after Lajos's brother who died in a Prisoner of War Camp, was a rambunctious little boy! I would be working in the garden with my mother, and then suddenly, Jozi would run by us in his birthday suit, laughing, and we would chase him yelling, "Jozi!" This was when he was three years old. He was mischievous, and it was his way of getting attention.

In 1947, the country was watching our world changing with the occupation by Russia. A lot of our freedoms were gradually disappearing. Businesses and properties were taken over by the government. Homeowners were notified that they had to pay rent to the government for the very homes they owned. There were attacks on our religious freedoms. The Secret Police known as the AVH, commissioned by Russia, were investigating Cardinal Mindszenty, our

Catholic leader, and they were listening to his services and sermons with the intention of arresting him. [7]

Joseph Stalin, Premier of Russia, believed the elimination of religion would divide the country and turn neighbors against neighbors. Informing on their neighbors, this helped control the population through fear. When these individuals were arrested on false accusations, they were prosecuted through confessions brought on by torture. This strategy assured the government was never wrong. They forced innocent people by torture to confess to allegations proving their guilt. If they confessed, they went through a brainwashing indoctrination process which left them never to be the same mentally again. This electric torture caused severe brain injuries. If they did not confess, then they were hanged, and relatives never knew what happened to their loved ones. Hungarians did not have individual rights.

Another manipulation happened on August 31, 1947. A National Election took place to place to replace the People's 1945 Election, when 57% of Hungarians defeated the Communist Party platform.[8] The Russian occupation in which Monarchy government changed to Socialism resulted in Hungarian resentment. The Russian Communist

---

[7] Cardinal Mindszenty was a Hungarian Cardinal of the Catholic Church, born Joseph Mindszenty in Hungary on March 29, 1892. He was ordained into the priesthood 1915, from November 27, 1944, to April 20, 1945, he was imprisoned by the Nazis. The Communist arrested Cardinal Mindszenty in Budapest on December 26, 1948, and he experienced 23 long years of persecution, suffering in isolation. Through all this he never wavered in his faith, hope and love of God. Cardinal Mindszenty departed his beloved Hungary on September 29, 1971, and settled in Vienna, Austria. He died in Vienna on May 6th, 1975, and is buried in Mariazell, Austria.

[8] Communist Party per the American Historical Association; The Communist Party is the only formal political organization permitted by the Soviet Constitution. Total control of political and economic life in the Soviet Union is centered in its hands. The party formulates all important policies as a one-party dictatorship.

Party had to show the world that an election favored Communism, and the people chose through their vote.⁹ ¹⁰

Matyas Menrath, Iren's father. Home Photo.

My father, Matyas Menrath, heard through his railroad contacts that the voting for the National Election in 1947 had two voting bins, the People's bin, which was a vote for the Communist Party, and a second bin for the Democratic Party. He learned that the second bin or Democratic Party was a collection of citizens' names who would be in jeopardy by the AVH and result in persecution. So, he directed us to vote for the Communist Party to stay out of danger. The results of the election in 1947 ushered in Communism which replaced Socialism and created government rule over the country. Everyone worked for Communism.

The Communist Party launched power and control over the Hungarian citizens, which included alliances and threats to remove elected politicians, resulting in control of the government. This was a gradual process where freedoms were gradually taken away, bit by bit, and the realization that the Communistic government was running the country. This created converts within the Communist Party, resulting in spies and the dismantling from within. This effort resulted in a coup d'état and the removal on May 31, 1947 of Ferenc Nagy, Prime Minister of Hungary.

---

[9] Monarchy government is a political system based upon the undivided sovereignty or rule of a single person.

[10] Socialism is a Marxist theory, a transitional social state between the overthrow of capitalism and the realization of communism, "socialism is the first stage of the worldwide transition to communism."

Cardinal Mindszenty, Wikipedia.

Cardinal Mindszenty, as a gesture to protect Hungarian religious life, created a St. Mary's Year, naming it Marian Year.[11] He traveled from city to city receiving thousands of attendees for his sermons. On August 15, 1947, a yearly religious event called "Mary Queen of Hungary" was established. This special celebration was when the Hungarian faithful came in the thousands. Cardinal Mindszenty preached to 70,000 Catholics in the city of Csongard on September 8, 1947, and 100,000 Catholics in Szombathely. Maria Suhajda, Lajos's mother, represented our family at the Szombathely sermon and reported a sea of Catholic attendees. The service was held outside of the church, and Cardinal Mindszenty had a sound system set up which was driven by batteries because the Communists cut power to areas upon their command. The crowd had a perimeter of soldiers and Secret Police.

In his sermon, he thanked all for coming, and he read from scripture and reminded everyone that someone had walked before them and suffered tyranny. He stated, "This man was spat on, whipped, and nailed to a cross. He is with you all, and his message is to keep your faith, love thy neighbor as he loves you and do not let division enter your house." Cardinal Mindszenty noticed the soldiers and said, "To the oppressors, I say to you, faith is stronger than oppression. As long as my countrymen are held prisoners within the borders of Hungary,

---

[11] Marian year is a designation given by the Catholic Church to calendar years in which Mary the mother of Jesus is celebrated.

the church bells will not ring until my brothers and sisters are free." (This passage would resonate with me later.)

The men of Hungary led a pilgrimage on September 14, 1947, when 100,000 men walked from Budapest to Mariaremete for the Penitential Pilgrimage.[12] September 20, 1947, 120,000 Catholics attended Cardinal Mindszenty's mass and sermon. Whenever possible, he would pray with the people.

These gatherings were highly embarrassing to the Communists, but they did not dare to ban them because of the high attendance. So, they tried other means to shut down the attendance. They refused to issue railroad tickets to those going to the "Mary Queen of Hungary" celebrations. They also reduced the number of railroad cars on the trains and reported that the trains were full. In some cases, traffic in entire cities was prohibited on the pretense of fictitious epidemics. The Communists would shut off water and power to the church facilities to control the Catholic gatherings.

The Secret Police, AVH terrorized our citizens and were on a mission to arrest Cardinal Mindszenty. They attended all his sermons and reviewed every word looking for a reason to arrest him. Cardinal Mindszenty knew his fate and dismissed opportunities to escape to Rome. He knew the torture awaiting him at the AVH Headquarters, located in Budapest on 60 Andrassy Street. He was steadfast in his decision to keep faith in God to help his Hungarian countrymen. He told his bereaved mother of 74 years, "A pastor of souls must stay with his flock and cannot flee like a hired servant. I know very well what my arrest and perhaps execution by the Communists would mean to you. I know this would break your heart. I have known for a long time, Mother, that grief would be your future. Please take comfort from the

---

[12] Penitential Pilgrimage the remembrance, reconciliation and healing from the Catholic Church's past sins committed against indigenous populations.

Blessed Mother whose heart was also pierced under the cross by the arrows of pain. For a long time, I have prayed to the Sorrowful Mother to give you the grace to accept God's will about my suffering and death." Cardinal Mindszenty concluded by saying, "With God's help, I was able to make you happy for a while. Now, you must take up your cross."

Cardinal Mindszenty's pastoral letter at the Bishops' Conference dated December 21, 1948, revealed his spiritual quality and leadership.[13] He wrote, "Everywhere and always, only that happens which God permits. Without His knowledge, not a single hair falls from our heads. The world can deprive us of many things, but it cannot take away our faith in Jesus Christ. Who can separate us from Him? Neither death nor life nor any other creature can separate us from the love of God, which is in Christ Jesus our Lord. (Romans 8:38-39). What he has told us is valid for all times. Do not worry about your life, or what you shall eat, or what you shall wear; your heavenly father will care for you. We cannot behave like men without faith or hope. Let us pray for those among us whose nerves are frayed by present events and who alarm and panic others around them. Let us pray that the bell of peace will toll in their tormented hearts, and that their way will be lighted by the Lord's question to his disciples on the stormy sea, why are you Fearful, O ye of little faith? Let us pray that the lesson of St. John Chrysostom may bring peace to our troubled hearts.[14] Although he was plagued by persecution and heavy crosses, nevertheless peace filled his heart, and he addressed his faithful from the harbor of Constantinople with these words." *'The waves roar and the storm rages, but we are not afraid because the rock of the Church cannot be crushed. Despite the hurricane around us, the Lord's*

---

[13] Bishops conference of 1948, had 21 members, the task of the Conference was to analyze, discuss and occasionally control the common pastoral duties of the Hungarian Catholic Bishops, and to coordinate the work of the Church.
[14] Saint John Chrysostom, an early Church Father who served as archbishop of Constantinople. He was known for his preaching and public speaking.

ship cannot sink. After all, what is there to fear? Death? My life is Christ and death would be my gain. Exile? The Lord has given us the whole world and its beauty. Confiscation? We did not bring anything into this world, and we can take nothing out of it. I despise that with which the world tries to frighten me. I laugh at the way the world tries to seduce me. I urge you to remain indomitably courageous and unfalteringly firm.' Cardinal Mindszenty continued, "Therefore, my friends, don't worry about tomorrow. Let us find our consolation in the Gospels and in the history of the world and our nation. Our Christian and Hungarian ancestors have never enjoyed soft lives. St. Paul, the apostle of suffering and persecution, sends us the message: *'For whatsoever things were written aforetime were written for our learning, that we through patience and comfort of the Scriptures might have hope.'* (Romans 15:4) …"

Mindszenty also wrote, "Priests, religious, and nuns are expected to give an example of standing firm at their posts. Our profession of faith must be a beacon to the faithful, to the members of other denominations, and to atheists. They must know more surely than ever before that, *'We are made a spectacle unto the world, and to angels, and to men.'* (1 Corinthians 4.9)" He wrote further with these words, "Let us be light shining in the darkness. According to our own abilities, let us each work with all our might to win the Kingdom of God which is the world of justice and grace. On our way to God, we cannot forget the words of Tertullian: *'The accusations of our accusers are our glory.'* Everything we have done has been to preserve the liberty of the Church, to safeguard our youth, to help our own suffering people, for peace, for higher spiritual values – and not for the reasons they accuse us . . ."[15]

His pastoral letter finished with these statements, "By the grace of God, we can rise to the heights of the Apostles who were willing to

---

[15] Tertullian was a prolific early Christian author from Carthage in the Roman province of Africa.

suffer flogging and ignominy for the love of Christ. Ours is the world of the Sermon on the Mount. '*Blessed are those who suffer persecution for justice' sake, for theirs is the Kingdom of Heaven. Blessed are you when men shall revile you and persecute you and shall say all manner of evil against you falsely, for my sake.*' (Matthew 5-10-11)" (*)

Cardinal Mindszenty arrest photo December 26. 1948, Wikipedia.

Cardinal Mindszenty was arrested December 26th, 1948, when an armed squad of Secret Police, AVH, broke into the archbishop's residence in Estergom, in front of his tearful mother.

We learned the truth of the propaganda sources through Radio Free Europe, the Hungarian Press, Szabadsag, and Magyar Radio. These sources reported false information about Cardinal Mindszenty as an enemy of the state and continually undermined the government. At this same time, in 1948 we could barely feed our family. We moved again, and this time we moved back to Lajos's mother's house in Dombegyhaz. Pista had bought his own home and had moved out, so we had room to move in and work toward the future. There was one threshing machine that Pista gave Lajos, and he made some money, but it was not enough to support the family through the winter. Pista secured several farm customers, and the machines that were loaned out were in poor condition and required repair. Lajos, having extensive mechanical experience repaired those threshing units, and as business picked up, Pista ordered more units. He paid Lajos very little for the required repairs which convinced Lajos to look for another job.

My mother came to visit us in Dombegyhaz, and she saw the stress of poverty and our living conditions. She told me that this was not good and that we should move to her home in Komlo. She said that in her town there was a mine where Lajos could secure a job, and life could be better. So, we moved to my parents' house. We took everything except the furniture, which was part of my dowry.[16] It stayed behind until we could settle and maintain a good income. It was not until 1950 that we picked up our furniture.

In 1948, Hungarians witnessed two elections. The 1947 National election was thrown out, and the Communists took over through ballot harvesting to win the 1948 election. As the first vote resulted in a Democratic majority, the second vote ushered in Communism. What did that mean for Hungary? Everyone worked for the government. Farmers had their farms taken away, businesses became the government's property, schools taught Socialism ideals, Hungary's history was changed to reflect Russian accomplishments and radio broadcasts reported propaganda instead of news. Freedom of the press was eliminated, newspapers like Szabadsag and Szabadnep along with others took over, and propaganda was the news of the day. Politicians were removed and replaced with Communist representatives. All profits went to the government and then forwarded to Russia/ Soviet Union. Russia infiltrated Hungarian industries, and that wealth was

---

[16] Dowry is the money, goods, or estate that a woman brings to her husband or his family in marriage.

shipped to Russia. Hungarian workers received quotas, and homeowners lost their homes and had to pay rent on their own property. Hungarian politicians were arrested and programmed to Communism, and the same happened to the teachers. The war had brought the largest tax burden on the citizens of Hungary with 22% of Gross National Product being paid to Russia/ Soviet Union. Anyone protesting was arrested, imprisoned or executed. Miklos Vilmos, the President of Zsolnay, a fine china manufacturer, instructed his children to leave Hungary, and he told his children that he was not giving up the family's business that was created from the ground up back in the 1800's. He was arrested and executed by the Russian/Soviet Union.

The Russian Kremlin assigned Matyas Rakosi, a puppet leader, as the Premier of Hungary, who received his orders from the Kremlin. The orders came into Ambassador Andropov's office on a direct line, known as the Red Phone. Andropov would instruct Rakosi and staff in a formal meeting the direction of Hungary's economy with an emphasis that led a propaganda spin. It was called the 5-Year Plan which covered every industry with propaganda of a better life. The promises were changed year by year, and the country was driven into economic disaster. Poverty was shared by all, and the middle class was eliminated.

The saving grace for Hungarians was the black market. A barter system developed, and households who had gardens would trade with neighbors for essentials. This was a tremendous help.

Chapter 6

Turbulent Times

Budapest Flying Club, Lajos was the instructor in 1948. Home photo.

We moved in with my mom and dad, Anna and Matyas. Lajos went to the Komlo Coal Mine, but they had no openings. So again, he searched for employment and heard of a flying club in Budapest that was looking for instructors. This was a government-formed flying club. He took the train to the interview, registered as an instructor and was hired in 1948. The airport was in Szeged, and he instructed civilian flight students at the Flying School Umbre. I stayed with my parents until the birth of my second son, Bela Suhajda, born July 7, 1949. One month later, Lajos came to pick us up and then took us to a furnished apartment in Aldju, which was a village next to Szeged. The Flying School Umbre shut down in October 1949, and we returned to my parents' home in Godisa.

Again, Lajos searched for a new job, but this time he had his flight instructor's credential, and he applied at Pecs Airport for an Airline named Magyar Soviet Vegi Forgalmi Tarsasag. He was hired two months later as the Airport Manager. The job opportunity came when the previous Airport Manager was held responsible for a crash that killed fourteen passengers and the pilot. On a foggy, cloudy day, the pilot upon take-off should have banked to the right, but he banked to the left into the adjacent mountain and crashed. He was disoriented and made a critical mistake. The Airport Manager was held responsible. He was tried and then imprisoned.

Lajos held the Chief Airport Manager's position from 1950 to 1952. It was a very happy time! We recovered our furniture and stayed in an apartment. We enjoyed going out, socializing with friends and going to the movies. Christmas was a true blessing filled with joy and happiness. We attended church to honor the Blessed Mary and the birth of her son Jesus. After church, we would go home and celebrate Christmas with our boys. In prior years we made the boys Christmas gifts such as knitted gloves, scarves, and wooden trucks, but now we bought toys and wrapped them. We decorated the Christmas tree with szaloncukor, a sweet fondant icing with a chocolate center wrapped in shiny colored foil. The boys had fun picking them off the Christmas tree. Those were very special times in our home in Hungary. We attended our first social New Year's Eve party! We danced and had a long-awaited celebration.

Jozef and Bela childhood photos. Home Photo.

Józef and Bela enjoyed the stability of our home and living status. The airport workers liked the boys and taught them mischievous things, like cursing. When they repeated the words, the workers would laugh, and the boys thought it was funny too. In 1951, the boys were ages four and two, and they loved being at the airport. I remember several incidents while the boys were growing up. For instance, when József would get angry and take his clothes off and then streak through the neighborhood. I would chase him to catch him before he went outside, but unfortunately, I was not always successful. Bela, on the other hand, would get mad and hold his breath until he turned blue and passed out. That scared the dickens out of me! My boys were headstrong, but I knew that someday they would be leaders.

During the time that Lajos was the Chief Airport Manager, he was to join the Communist Party. He always put it off and used the busy workload as his excuse. The truth was that he hated the Communist Party and believed if he joined the Party, it would be condoning the death of his brother József, who died in a Russian-controlled Prisoner of War Camp. This proved to be a major mistake.

In June 1951, I was pregnant with my third child, Laszlo, and we faced a major crisis. Lajos was fired from his job while he was on medical leave. What happened was that Lajos was walking with a friend, who was a radio operator in the Airport tower, and they were headed to a fellow worker's winery. It was harvesting season in the fall of the year, and they were going to drink some squeezed sweet grape wine. As they were walking home, a motorcycle operator was reaching for his drink in the side compartment of his motorcycle, and he hit Lajos, throwing him twenty feet in the air, which broke his right leg. As I was waiting for Lajos to come home, the day turned into night with no word. At first, I thought they were caught up talking, or perhaps they drank too much and decided to sleep there. Anyway, I went to bed and periodically awoke to look at the clock. At 1:00 a.m. and 3:00 a.m., and he was still not home. In the morning, Lajos's mom, Marika and I ate breakfast, and then we went outside to feed our animals. Lajos's friend, Sandor came by early and was waiting for signs that I was up. He saw us in the backyard and came over to report Lajos was in the hospital with a broken leg. He gave me the phone number of the hospital and told me to go to Lajos's office and to phone the hospital. The nurse at the hospital reported his condition, and then Marika and I took the bus to the hospital to visit him. We arrived and walked into the room seeing that his face had bruises with his right leg in a cast.

I reported the accident to the Headquarters in Budapest and told them that he would be in the hospital for one week and that a substitute Airport Manager would be needed. An Interim Airport Manager was assigned until Lajos was well enough to go back to work. After a week went by, Lajos was released to home care. He had to remain at home for one week and then resume his job.

During this timeline, the Airport bus driver, whose job was to follow an assigned route, and pick-up, plus to drop off passengers to and from the airport to the surrounding villages, was continually late. He had been warned previously by Lajos. The driver promised to stop drinking during his shift but continued his bad habit with the Interim Airport Manager. He stopped at the local winery to drink wine after he completed his route, but before returning the bus. On this day he asked Lajos and me to take our son, József on his route. We knew József liked the bus, and he thought József would enjoy it. We agreed, and Lajos told him to return after his route which he agreed to do.

The Interim Manager noticed the driver was tardy, and he came to our apartment to report his concern, "Mr. Suhayda, the driver is late, and I am concerned." Lajos explained, "He has on occasion stopped at a local winery after his route. I have warned him about this several times. He will return in an hour or so." The Interim Manager feared, "If anything should happen with the new bus, I will be responsible. If he isn't back by 6:00 pm, which is one hour past his scheduled time of 5:00 pm, I will write him up per Airport Policy." When 6:00 p.m. came, he wrote the bus driver up for violating his duties and called the police. The police went to several wineries neighboring the airport and found the bus driver. He was arrested and taken to the Police Department and driven to the hospital for a blood test which was ordered. After he was released, the bus driver headed directly to the airport and to our apartment. He walked into our home and went directly to our bedroom where Lajos was lying in bed with his leg propped up. In his anger, he yelled about how he was arrested, "Look what the hospital has done to me! They took blood, and you reported me to the police. This is a serious charge, and I could lose my job. I have a family and three kids, and because I had your boy on the bus, you turned me in!" Lajos replied, "No, I did not report you! The Interim Airport Manager did, and he is in charge. I warned you today, and you have been warned many times not to drink while on duty, but you stopped at the winery anyway instead of returning the bus." He replied, "I don't believe you! You wrote me up! I'm going to get you for this. You just watch and see." He left in a huff. The bus driver did not lose his job. He was a Red Book holder, a member of the Communist Party.[17]

The winery manager's wife knew us because her husband worked at the airport. She had already brought Jozi home before the bus driver came to the apartment. She told us the driver was so drunk that she did not believe it was safe for Jozi to ride with him. This caused a major issue because the driver thought Lajos had written him up for trying to drive József while intoxicated. Lajos told him that he did not write him up, but the driver did not believe him. The bus driver wrote a letter to the Airport Headquarters reporting Lajos for using the bus for personal reasons and for stealing fuel from the airport.

These unsubstantiated accusations resulted in Lajos being fired and charges being brought up against him for his arrest. A trial was set for

---

[17] Communist Red book holder was governed by the Hungarian Socialist Workers' Party, which was under the influence of the Soviet Union, which was agreed that after the war Hungary was to be included in the Soviet sphere of influence, which existed until 1989.

the charges. Lajos went to the Communist Union Board, and he met with the manager and explained what happened. The Union leader said, "This is a misunderstanding. In the Red Book, it is stated that an employee cannot be fired while on medical leave. I will go to Budapest to talk with the management of Magyar Soviet Vegi Forgalmi Tarsasag Headquarters and resolve the matter. Come back in two weeks, and I will report my results." I was determined to help Lajos! An injustice was done, a false accusation had been taken as truth, and I had to take action to correct a wrong. I took the train to Budapest and went to the Airport Headquarters to report the false accusations. I walked into the office and asked for Mr. Bochkarov, a Russian Executive, and in turn, I was met by the Vice President, Olga Bochkarov. I reported the story and emphatically stated, "The bus driver lied, there is no truth to the accusations, and it needs to be investigated. You can't fire an Airport Manager based on accusations without investigating. Find the truth!" Olga replied, "Het, (the Russian word for NO, pronounced Nyet), the decision has been made, and the court will determine what is true and what is not." I became angry and made a firm reply, "The Hungarian people were told that the Russians were our liberators, who were bringing justice to our country, and this is the type of injustice you are bringing?" She got very angry and said, "Het! How dare you say that to me! Russia liberated Hungary and you should be grateful." I replied, "Liberated Hungary from whom? We should be liberated from Russia!" She angrily interjected, "I see you are pregnant. If you weren't, I would have you arrested! You will have to move out of the apartment because that will be turned over to the new Airport Manager. So, get your fat ass out of my office!" As I was leaving, I yelled, "Russia liberated Hungarians from our freedoms. You should be ashamed of yourself!" I slammed the door.

On the way back home on the train, I sat in front of a pregnant young lady, about my age, dressed in shabby clothes with the "world on her shoulders". I started small talk with her, "I don't mean to pry, but when is your due date?" She answered, "I have one month to go." I responded, "So do I!" I introduced myself, "I am Iren Suhajda, I am going to Pecs." She excitedly replied, "I am Kriszta Borbely, and I am going to Paksi." I tried to make her feel comfortable. I put my bag on the floor and told her to use it as a footstool. I warmed up to her and told her about the war years. Then she opened up to me. During the Russian advancement into Hungary, her parents hid her, but the Russians found her hiding place, and they took her away. She was passed around by the troops, raped many times, beaten, and then ended up breaking her leg. They did not get her medical help to reset the bone, and so it healed crooked. This resulted in her walking with a limp. She had not seen her parents for seven years, and she was afraid of what they would think of her. Her parents lived in Paksi which was two stops away. She said that her parents would be at the train station to meet her. As the train pulled into the small station, she was looking around and finally spotted her parents. Kriszta thanked me for keeping her company. I felt sorry for her as she got her belongings and limped off the train. Her parents were so overjoyed to see her! They hugged and kissed her with simple joy and happiness in their hearts that she was now home with them once again. I realized that this situation could have been me if Captain Rothenfelder had not taken me along with the squadron's surrender to the American Forces in Germany. Tears gathered in my eyes as I watched them walk away from the station.

Upon my return, I told Lajos that we were ordered to vacate the apartment because it was to be turned over to the new Airport Manager. Lajos and I returned to the Union Leader's Office and reported the order that was given. He replied, "No, if they are terminating Lajos's employment, they must assign a new apartment to him. That is also in the Red Book. It is good that you came to tell me what was said. I am going to Budapest tomorrow, and I will address all these points. Come to my office in one week, on next Friday, and I will report the situation." We were very grateful and said that we would be back that next Friday.

The Union Leader went to Budapest and met up with the local Union Leader, and they both went to Magyar Soviet Vegi Forgalmi Tarsasag Headquarters and met with President, Mr. Bochkarov. They were escorted into the conference room, exchanged some pleasantries, and the Union Leaders explained why they had come. They cited the statutes of the Communist Red Book stating employees cannot be fired while on medical leave, and if someone is fired or replaced, the company is mandated to find them equal living quarters with the separation. This was the law. Mr. Bochkarov's demeanor changed, and he became irate, "Het! Who are you to tell me what I can and cannot do? You get out of my office, or I'll contact my connections and have you fired!"

We returned the next week. We were greeted by the local Union Leader and asked to sit down in front of his large oak desk. The Budapest Chief Union Leader made the trip for this important meeting. He paced back and forth, looking at Lajos. He paused, looked at me, and he said, "Do you know who Mr. Bochkarov is?" I said, "Yes, he is the President of the airport where my husband works." He inquired, "Do you know he is Russian?" I replied, "Of course, I know he is Russian." He looked at Lajos, and while pausing, he asked, "Have you ever tried to piss into the wind? (In pausing again) I am looking at the most important man in Hungary!" He threw the Red Communist Book on his desk and said, "Because of you, the Communist handbook is being changed. Workers now can be fired while on medical leave, and the firing organization does not have to assign new quarters for the fired individual. I recommend you secure a good lawyer. I can recommend an intelligent young Russian attorney who can help you with this case."

Lajos shook his head, "NO! If I have to get an attorney, I want a Hungarian attorney. I don't trust Russians." The Chief Union Leader replied, "No, you need a Russian attorney who knows how the prosecutors think. He is meticulous, energetic, and very knowledgeable. I recommend Yuri Kaminski. He will pick them apart because this happened under the old Red Book Law and will be tried that way. The prosecution will be dealing with hate because you are not a Red Book Communist Party member. You are a working-class member, and they want to make an example out of you. Don't let them succeed." After a few minutes of thought, Lajos agreed and said, "Alright, I understand. I will accept your recommendation." The Chief Union Leader then added, "I will have Yuri contact you this Monday. He speaks fluent Hungarian and Russian and will do a very good job for you. I want the Communist Red Book protected, and he will be winning your case."

Monday arrived, and we met Yuri Kaminski at the office of the Union Leader and discussed the case in their conference room. Yuri was a young attorney and highly intelligent. He explained what the prosecutor would try to do, "The prosecutor will go after the biggest accusation, which is the stealing of airport fuel." (directing his questions to Lajos) "Do you own a vehicle?" Lajos replied, "No, I do not." Yuri's next question was, "Do you own a tractor or any piece of equipment that requires diesel fuel?" "No, I do not." Lajos answered. Yuri, looking at both of us, continued, "Good, we will catch them with inventory reports and signed fuel receipts which will have the bus driver's name on each. It will prove that there were no signed receipts by you. This audit will prove all the fuel is accounted for." I asked Yuri, "What will happen if Lajos is found guilty?" Yuri said, "He will be sentenced to Siberia for a number of years. I am not concerned about that because once I prove that no fuel was stolen, the prosecution will have no basis. As for the other charge of using the bus for personal reasons, I will map out the bus driver's route and question him if that is the route taken on a daily basis. He will answer that question with a yes, and I will introduce the stop where you were getting off for your doctor's visit and ask him if that is a deviation from his route." Looking at Lajos, Yuri asked, "This was a new bus, correct?" Lajos answered with confidence, "Yes." Yuri asked, "Was the bus put into service immediately, or were there trial trips conducted for the driver to acquaint himself with the bus?" Lajos informed Yuri, "We had a meeting to discuss a training trip, and the bus driver suggested driving to his brother's home, which was a twenty-minute ride. I agreed." Yuri commented, "Ok, I will ask this question in a certain way as a yes or a no question."

Chapter 7

The Trial

The case was strategized and set. We entered the court, and we were afraid that an accusation could result in a miscarriage of justice. Yuri briefed us, and in seeing how nervous we were, he calmed us by saying, "The audit was completed, and every liter of fuel is accounted for and recorded. The prosecution has no case. The judge will have no recourse but to dismiss."

It was January, 1952. A very sunny, chilly day. Outside, the snow reflected the sunlight, but inside, the courtroom was dark and scary. The judge's bench was two steps up from the floor with a prosecution table and a defense table on both sides of the judge. There was no jury. Only the judge decided the case. The seats in the courtroom were filled with onlookers. I saw both Olga and President Buchkarov with his entourage watching. The Judge was introduced to the court as Judge Skotnovski presiding, and then the judge announced, "The court is now in session. The State versus Suhajda on the count of stealing fuel from Magyar Soviet Vegi Forgalmi Tarsasag Airlines and using an airport bus for personal purposes. How do you plead?" Yuri stood up and pleaded, "Not guilty!" The judge looked at the prosecuting table and informed Mr. Debrenkov to begin his opening statement. Mr. Debrenkov stood and stated, "The state will prove through eyewitness testimony that the defendant stole company fuel for his own personal use, and he used the company bus for his own purposes." Judge Skotnovski then turned to Mr. Yuri Kaminski and asked for his opening statement. Yuri stood up and stated, "The defense will prove the charges presented were accusations with no merit and initiated as a revenge motive for a disciplinary write-up."

After hearing the opening statements, the judge wanted Mr. Debrenkov to call his first witness. Mr. Debrenkov stood and called his witness, "I call Mr. Haggaduc, the bus driver to the stand." The stand was located to the left of the judge in front of the prosecution table, he was sworn in and seated. Mr. Debrenkov began, "You are the bus driver for the Pecs Airport, is that correct?" Haggaduc replied, "Yes Sir." Mr. Debrenkov continued, "You have reported witnessing the theft of diesel fuel from the airport fuel terminal by the defendant, Mr. Suhajda. How many times did you witness him stealing diesel fuel?" Mr. Haggaduc replied, "I saw Mr. Suhajda on three occasions filling up an 11-liter fuel can at the terminal in the month of September." Mr. Debrenkov asked, "The airport acquired a new bus, is that correct?" Haggaduc replied, "Yes." Debrenkov inquired, "Did the defendant use this new bus acquired in September for his own personal purposes to transport his pregnant wife for doctor visits?" Haggaduc answered, "Yes!" Debrenkov said, "I have no further questions. It is your witness."

Yuri asked, "Mr. Haggaduc, when you fill your bus up with fuel, do you sign a fuel chit?" Haggaduc replied, "Yes, we always sign a fuel chit." "What days did you witness this theft?" retorted Yuri. "It was in September, but I do not remember the dates." explained Haggaduc. Yuri faced the judge and claimed, "Your Honor, I present evidence of an audit on the company's fuel usage in the month of September, showing a beginning inventory, purchases, and signed fuel chits with an ending balance being exactly correct, proving there was no theft that took place. All of the signed fuel receipts have Mr. Haggaduc's signature on them, proving the accusations were made up and a complete lie." Yuri continued his questioning, "When was the new bus purchased?" Mr. Haggaduc stated, "The beginning of September,

1951." Yuri inquired, "Was there a meeting to trial the bus to acquaint yourself with the handling?" Haggaduc replied, "Yes." Yuri continued, "Did you suggest traveling to your brother's home which was twenty miles away?" He again replied, "Yes." Advancing with more questions, Yuri asked, "Did Mr. Suhajda ride with you on this test run?" Haggaduc stated, "Yes." Yuri handed Mr. Haggaduc a map and commanded, "Look at this map and tell me if this is the route you take on a daily basis from the airport and back?" Haggaduc looked and paused for a moment studying it and informed Yuri, "Yes, that is correct." Yuri, focusing on the map evidence, said, "Do you see the X on that map?" Haggaduc responded, "Yes." As Yuri pressed further, "Did you know that is the medical center Mrs. Suhajda went to on your bus and the stop that you just confirmed is on your daily route? Did she get off at that location when she rode on your bus to the doctor?" Haggaduc answered abruptly, "Yes!" As Yuri led with his questions more intensely, he then asked, "Mr. Haggaduc, have you stopped on your return from your route at a winery before returning your bus?" "On occasion, I have stopped for a glass of wine, yes." Mr. Haggaduc responded annoyingly. Going further, Yuri interjected, "Were you warned by Mr. Suhajda, Airport Manager, not to stop to drink while in possession of the airport bus?" "Yes." It was noted that Mr. Haggaduc responded with a definite yes. "You violated his order and Mr. Antonov, the Interim Airport Manager, wrote you up. Were you aware of that?" retorted Yuri. "No! it was Mr. Suhajda," Haggaduc tried to claim. Yuri stated with confidence, "No, it was Mr. Antonov, and thank you for admitting your motive. You brought accusations out of revenge, but to the wrong person!" Yuri turned to face the judge and said, "Your Honor, I submit this case be dismissed." The judge with a stern look turned to the prosecution table, raised his gavel, and slammed it, saying, "Case dismissed!"

We were ecstatic and thanked Yuri for his fine work. We heard rumbling in the gallery, and the prosecuting attorney was talking to Mr. Bochkarov. He came over to Lajos and me and said, "Het! Mr. Bochkarov said this trial means nothing, and you are still fired."

The Communist Red Book is specific about firing employees. The company must find an exact lodging replacement for the dismissed employee. Mr. Bochkarov violated the rules, and no one dared to address the point due to his position of power. We went to City Hall and explained our situation and our need for new housing. They took us to some run-down houses showing what was available. One house had a 3-foot hole in the ceiling, another had a missing front door, and they all looked like condemned houses ready to be torn down. The Vice President, Olga Buchkarov, did give us permission to stay at the airport apartment until our third child was born. On February 2, 1952, our son Laszlo was brought into this world of turmoil and uncertainty. We forged on after his birth and found an apartment in Siklos. It was run down, but there were no holes in the ceiling, and we had a front door that locked. Life was now on a new path towards security and happiness for our little family.

Chapter 8
From Hard Times, To Family

When Lajos's leg healed, he went to City Hall and applied to secure a job. He requested an aviation position based on his experience, and at that time he had been blacklisted from aviation positions. According to the Communist Party Lajos had to take whatever position they gave to him. Communism law dictated what job you were required to accept without rejection. Lajos was assigned to a transmission shop job in Pecs repairing cars and trucks. He took the train every day from Siklos to Pecs and had to work at his designated job for six months as a punishment from the trial.

After six months, Lajos decided to get his truck driver's license to haul trees for the Forestry Department. The forestry job kept him away for six days out of the week from his family. His duty was to load the trees and haul the wood to the train station for shipment. He started the trucking job in September 1952, and he worked there into the winter. After his evening ended, Lajos was responsible for draining the water from all the trucks' radiators because the sub-zero temperature could expand the water, destroy the radiator and crack the trucks' blocks. One evening, he was the last driver to pull in when the Maintenance Chief told Lajos to drain all the trucks' water. While he was working, a truck arrived late, but it parked behind the building without reporting in. When Lajos finished his work, he left for home. The late driver did not tell him that he had parked in the back of the building, and unfortunately, that truck was not drained. Overnight the temperature dropped way below freezing, and the radiator seams cracked as the ice expanded. Lajos was fired in January 1953, and our cycle of hardships returned once again. If he had his Communist Red Book, Lajos would not have been fired, only reprimanded.

Since we needed to find a secure environment for all of us, we took the children to Godisa to stay with my mother and father. We were hoping that the New Year would bring us a better life. It was February 1953, and I found out that I was once again pregnant. Unhappily there were complications, and I had to have surgery to regain my health. Lajos went to Komlo, and he finally secured a job in the mines. So, we continued to stay with my parents. I returned from the hospital, and in the Spring, we returned to Siklos and collected our furniture. Things started to look up as we were able to move to a rented house of our own.

The house was a pleasant one, and we were finally at a home that we could appreciate. A four-room house, consisting of two bedrooms, a living room, and a kitchen with an outhouse. The house was set on a half-acre that was fenced in with a barn. It allowed us to have chickens, a rooster, pigs, and a garden. My mother and I planted a large garden behind the house on the left side of the backyard. We planted corn, onions, garlic, peppers, carrots, cucumbers, tomatoes, radishes, lettuce, cabbage and peas. We used the garden to barter with neighbors. One of our neighbors had a cow, so we would trade vegetables for milk. My sons, Jozi and Bela, would walk over to the neighbor's house and drop off vegetables in order to pick up a container of milk. They both would grab a handle on the milk container as they walked home.

Dingo our family dog, a great hunter, loyal and loving pet.

The boys would play in the back with a soccer ball. Grandpa built a pigeon coupe, and the boys would watch the pigeons grow and fly. A secret we had was that we served pigeon for supper, but we called it chicken. One of our neighbors would take the boys out for horse and wagon rides. This gentleman had two horses that he hooked up to his wagon, and the boys sat along with the neighbor while they drove the team.

Laci loved horses and would sit on a wooden horse with a rope attached to Dingo, our dog. Dingo sat patiently in front of Laci as he pretended that he was driving his team of horses with a green wooden whip, made of leather lash, that continually came untied. He would pick up the leather lash, run into the house, give it to Grandpa Menrath and say, "Tie it, tie it." Grandpa would tie it back on, and then Laci would run back out and continue his wagon ride! But within two minutes, he would be back in the house asking Grandpa to tie it again. This always brought laughter to us all.

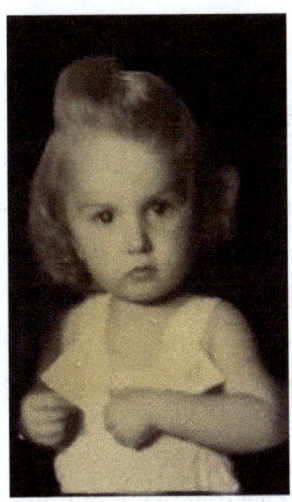

Laci at age two, 1954. Home photo.

I always wanted a little girl, and I used to dress Laci up in dresses. I grew his hair to shoulder length, and as it curled, I put ribbons in it. Everyone thought Laci was a little girl. At night time, I brushed his hair which would always be a tangled mess because of his boyhood play. Laci would scream and cry from all the tugging and pulling on his hair. My mother would always say, "What are you doing with that child? He is a boy. Let him be a boy!" I would agree and say, "I know, I will in time. Just let me enjoy him a little longer as a girl!" One day we were taking a walk in the neighborhood, and a neighbor lady friend, Judka walked up to us. We were talking when Laci started squirming while tugging on my skirt.

He said, "I have to pee pee." I replied, "Go over to that bush and pee there." Judka watched as Laci went over, pulled up his dress and peed. Judka said, "Oh my goodness! I thought Laci was a girl." That is when he became a true-blue boy!

When Jozi was six years old he started school in the village. He was very intelligent, and we noticed leadership qualities in him. Protective of his brothers, even though Bela and he would have disagreements, he would always protect them from others. At the school there was a boy, Gruber, who bullied other boys. When Bela was just starting school, Gruber started picking on him on his way home from school. Jozi stepped in and defended Bela. There were cuts, scrapes and black eyes on the boys. Being concerned, I exclaimed to Jozi, "Look at both of you! What happened?" Jozi replied, "Gruber, a bully at school, was picking on Bela, so I took care of him! You should see his face." Justice was served, and the harassment stopped.

Bela was a tough-minded little boy. He was stubborn in his ways, and he never backed down from situations. He fought Gruber at the beginning while taking his lumps. His headstrong behavior made him independent, not needing assistance from his brother. I saw the beginning of a leader in Bela. When he set his mind on something, he wanted total control. As we were moving to our new home, he demanded to stay with Grandma and Grandpa Menrath. Bela was so upset about not staying at their home that he held his breath until he turned blue and passed out. Lajos and I held our position and did not enable him to get his way. Once we had settled into our home, he was fine.

Lajos had friends come over with their motorcycles that needed tuning up, and he did mechanical repairs. It was a way to get extra money to help support our family. His mechanical experience made him the man to go to for fixing any engines. The Communist Government was hard work with little pay. Since we lived in a third world country, everyone was owned by the Government. We maintained ourselves with our working role wages that were barely enough to sustain our family. It fell on our ingenuity to secure additional ways to provide for our family. We bartered a particular skill in exchange for skills that our neighbors possessed. By bartering with our neighbors with the vegetables in our garden, we were able to have milk, honey and other things to save money and provide for our family.

Lajos would go hunting in the forest behind our house with Dingo, my father's Visla dog. It was great when he brought home rabbits and, on some occasions, a turkey. Dingo was the boys' childhood dog who loved all of us. He was smart and very patient with the boys' boisterous play. His hunting tactics were exceptional. Dingo would quietly search, point out prey, and after the kill, he would retrieve the prey. Dingo was so loved!

Chapter 9
Államvédelmi Hatóság, AVH

On March 5, 1953, Joseph Stalin died, and his successor was Nikita Khrushchev. Imre Nagy was appointed Chairman of the Council of Ministers in Hungary, and he reported to Matyas Rakosi, General Secretary and puppet leader for the Communist Government of Hungary that was strictly controlled by the Kremlin. The Russian Ambassador to Hungary was Yuri Andropov, who was appointed in July 1954, and he held an office in the AVH, *Államvédelmi Hatóság, Andrassy ut 60, Budapest*. The Hungarian Secret Police communicated with the Kremlin and received orders to pass on to the Hungarian Government. The Five-Year Plan, dictated by Russia, was to turn Hungary into a predominantly industrial country.[18] Hungary, being an agriculture country, was doomed to economic disaster and poverty. Ambassador Yuri Andropov reported those orders to the appropriate powers. Rakosi was a puppet ruler who was extremely disliked by Hungarians. Rakosi was in charge of the AVH Hungarian Secret Police, and Laszlo Rajk was the man who had organized the AVH, which was an instrument of fear. The personnel were sociopaths who enjoyed torture and murder. They were ruthless and were responsible for over 100,000 innocent citizen deaths. The AVH organization was designed after the Russian KGB. The AVH's whole purpose was to administer fear into the population in any way that they could. Any

---

[18] The Five-Year plan was drafted by Russia and mandated to Hungary through Ambassador Andropov who received the economic plan controlling all Hungarian industries by the Kremlin which mandated the Hungarian Communist Party to follow and was the instrument that made Hungary's infrastructure to fail.

citizen report would trigger action to pick up the individual, whether innocent or guilty, in their black limousine, the terror on wheels, which made many stops. The individuals who were picked up were beaten and tortured by using electric shock, and they were administered other vile means. They were tried in a mock court where they confessed or claimed their innocence. The truth did not matter to the AVH. All the victims had a chance to confess to whatever crime the fear machine imposed, or they were tortured until they confessed. If they did not confess, they were tried and hung in the basement gallows. If they confessed, they went through brainwashing in prison and returned to their families as a different person, never to be the same.

On one occasion, Mr. Horvath, a hog farmer, raised pigs for the market. He had a quota issued by the government to raise pigs with 95% going to the government and the other 5% kept for his family. He did not receive compensation for feed, veterinary or equipment expenses. He had to manage that through his 5% share. On one fall day in September 1955, he had a big get-together, and he invited his neighbors. The men took part in slaughtering one of Mr. Horvath's pigs for food for the winter. The wives made Hungarian sausages: Kolbasz, Csemege, Cserkesz, Gyulai, Csabai and Hurka. The next-door neighbor was invited, but he did not attend. He watched the jubilation and the work being put into this neighborhood gathering. This man became jealous and reported Mr. Horvath to the AVH for slaughtering one of the government's quota pigs. At 2:00 a.m., the AVH went to the farm, arrested him and took him into the village square where he was hung. The AVH placed a sign stating, "Horvath, a criminal to the State, caught stealing and butchering a government pig." Such a tragic end to a good and respected man who was killed over a jealous neighbor.

Chapter 10

Hungarian Revolution

The Budapest University Engineering students studied and witnessed atrocities committed by the AVH. They monitored the 5-Year Plan that came into Hungary through Ambassador Andropov's Red Phone. Khrushchev's orders to the Rakosi regime were to execute the 5-Year Plan.

The students drafted a 16-points manifesto document calling out a list of demands on behalf of the people. All the points were based on historical atrocities that they had witnessed or studied:

1. We demand the immediate evacuation of all Soviet troops, in conformity with the provisions of the Peace Treaty.

2. We demand the election by secret ballot of all Party members from top to bottom, and of new officers for the lower, middle, and upper echelons of the Hungarian Workers Party. These officers shall convene a Party Congress as early as possible to elect a Central Committee.

3. A new Government must be constituted under the direction of Imre Nagy: all criminal leaders of the Stalin-Rakosi era must be immediately dismissed.

4. We demand a public enquiry into the criminal activities of Mihaly Farkas and his accomplices. Matyas Rakosi, Prime Minister of Hungary, who is the person most responsible for crimes of the recent past as well as for our country's ruin, must be returned to Hungary for trial before a people's tribunal.

5. We demand that general elections by universal, secret ballots are held throughout the country to elect a new National Assembly, with all political parties participating. We demand that the right of workers to strike be recognized.

6. We demand revision and re-adjustment of Hungarian-Soviet and Hungarian-Yugoslav relations in the field of politics, economics, and cultural affairs, on a basis of complete political and economic equality, and of non-interference in the internal affairs of one by the other.

7. We demand the complete reorganization of Hungary's economic life under the direction of specialists. The entire economic system, based on a system of planning, must be re-examined in the light of conditions in Hungary and in the vital interest of the Hungarian people. *

8. Our foreign trade agreements and the exact total of reparations that can never be paid must be made public. We demand to be precisely informed of the uranium deposits in our country, on their exploitation and on the concessions to the Russians in this area. We demand that Hungary have the right to sell her uranium freely at world market prices to obtain hard currency.

9. We demand complete revision of the norms operating in industry and an immediate and radical adjustment of salaries in accordance with the just requirements of workers and intellectuals. We demand a minimum living wage for workers.[19]

10. We demand that the system of distribution be organized on a new basis and that agricultural products be utilized in a rational manner. We demand equality of treatment for individual farms.

---

[19] Hungary was devastated with a 22% tax on GNP, that destroyed Hungary"s economy which led to the seventh point.

11. We demand reviews by independent tribunals of all political and economic trials as well as the release and rehabilitation of the innocent. We demand the immediate repatriation of prisoners of war, (World War II), and of civilian deportees to the Soviet Union, including prisoners sentenced outside Hungary.

12. We demand complete recognition of freedom of opinion and expression, of freedom of the press and of the radio, as well as the creation of a daily newspaper for the MEFESZ Organization (Hungarian Federation of University and College Students' Association)

13. We demand that the statue of Stalin, the symbol of Stalinist tyranny and political oppression, be removed as quickly as possible and be replaced by a monument in memory of the martyred freedom fighters of 1848-49. [20][21]

14. We demand the replacement of emblems foreign to the Hungarian people by the old Hungarian arms of Kossuth. We demand that March 15th be declared a national holiday and that October 6th be a day of national mourning on which schools will be closed.

15. The students of the Technology University of Budapest declare unanimously their solidarity with the workers and students of Warsaw and Poland in their movement toward national independence.

---

[20] The students wanted all Soviet Union's insignias removed. This was to be in remembrance of those who died in the village of Magyarovar. Men, women, and children were murdered for asking to remove the hammer and sickle from the Hungarian flag.

[21] Hungarian Freedom Fighters were organized militias to fight; local Hungarian communist leaders and AVH Secret Police, for political, economic, and social demands.

16. The students of the Technology University of Budapest will organize, as rapidly as possible, local branches of MEFESZ, and they have decided to convene at Budapest, on Saturday, October 27, 1956, in a Youth Parliament at which all the nation's youth shall be represented by their delegates.

AVH Magyarovar massacres, Life Magazine 1956.

This manifesto was distributed to the working class of Hungary, and the nation agreed and rallied around the document setting off the Revolution. Twenty thousand protesters, including students from the Technical Institute marched to the Parliament building and were joined by workers totaling two hundred thousand. They toppled a 30-foot statue of Stalin at Hero's Square.

The delegation of students went to the Hungarian Radio station to broadcast the sixteen points and were detained by the AVH, and the mass of students and workers outside the radio station demanded their delegation be released. The AVH shot into the crowd killing many students. The Hungarian soldiers who were dispatched to watch over the demonstration saw the AVH response of shooting into the crowd and returned fire, killing many AVH shooters. Ambassador Andropov watched the events from his second-floor office and became very angry. He picked up his Red Phone that was a direct line to the Kremlin and reported the revolution. By order of the First Secretary, Nikita Khrushchev, Ambassador Andropov was recalled and ordered to take an immediate flight to Moscow.

The next day, a top priority meeting took place with Ambassador Andropov reporting the Radio Station demonstration and Hungarian soldiers firing on the AVH police. First Secretary Khrushchev angrily yelled out, "This revolution will be put down, (as he slammed his shoe five times on the top of his desk), and Hungary will be made an example for all occupied countries to see."

Khrushchev's plan started with recalling all Russian soldiers who were sympathetic to Hungarians. Some soldiers had married Hungarian women and were immediately removed from the ranks of the military.

Hungary, seeing the withdrawal of troops, believed they could be liberated. They reached out to the West for help. Efforts were made to address the United Nations to be recognized as a free country. Imre Nagy declared Hungary's removal from the Warsaw Pact that allowed Russia/ Soviet Union to occupy the Eastern bloc European countries.[22]

300 Russian tank assault on Hungary, Wikipedia.

Khrushchev's plan was to bring down the Siberian Army, the army that defeated the Germans during the winter advancement by the Germans into Moscow. They were ruthless, and that was needed to put down the revolution. Khrushchev would negotiate with Imre Nagy, who was chosen by Hungary to lead them. Rakosi exiled to Russia for asylum and was replaced. Negotiations were progressing with more freedoms being discussed.

---

[22] Warsaw Pact provided for a unified military command and the systematic ability to strengthen the Soviet hold over other participating countries.

The international pulse welcomed Khrushchev's benevolent efforts for peace.

When the Siberian army arrived through Ukraine at the border of Hungary, they were ordered to advance and destroy. Four thousand T-54 tanks rolled into Hungary in strategic locations and were positioned to annihilate and destroy key cities. Khrushchev's plan had worked, and the devastation of Budapest and other major cities like Debrecen, Miskolc, Gyor, and Pecs were the final results.

During this planned invasion, Hungarians organized into revolutionary militias, better known as Freedom Fighters, and attacked Communist leaders and the AVH. The AVH building, at 60 Andrassy Street, was overrun, and AVH policemen were captured and hung. Prisoners were released, including Cardinal Mindszenty.

Radio Hungary was free to report the truth, not propaganda, but it was short-lived. The Revolution was put down on November 4, 1956. The Russians patrolled the Hungarian borders and placed land minefields to prevent any escape. They shot people and families trying to flee their country. The Freedom Fighters fought on till November 10th, when many were killed, and others were arrested and executed.

There were many examples of Freedom Fighters being executed for their brave actions, like Istvan Baber who was arrested for taking part in the uprising with an attack on the party headquarters and participating in the attack on the AVH Headquarters that resulted in an AVH officer being killed. Baber was tried and sentenced to death for his participation. *

Another example happened on November 2, 1956, when Istvan Micsinai, a Freedom Fighter, joined the 20th District National Guard and as a guardsman, witnessed a comrade shoot and kill an AVH officer. The comrade escaped across the border, and Micsinai was held responsible and was executed for witnessing the atrocity. *

A third example was on October 23, 1956, when Laszlo Kovacs, who was accepted as the Commander of the Corvin Passage Group, took part in the Radio Building attack. On October 29, his delegation was received by Imre Nagy when he presented the demands of the Corvin Passage Group. The demands would guarantee the country's independence with a negotiated withdrawal of Russian/Soviet troops from Hungary, plus an end to the Communist one-party system. On November 4th, he took part in the fight against Russian/Soviet troops, and after the defeat of the Revolution, he continued the resistance movement, was arrested and then sentenced to death. *

The uprising killed 2,500 Hungarians and 700 Soviet Army soldiers and compelled 200,000 Hungarians to refugee abroad.

Radio Hungary reported the events of Russian devastation and appealed to the West to help the Hungarian nation, pleading with the sound of explosions in the background. The announcer kept pleading until he was shot and killed on air.

Chapter 11

The Escape

In the summer of 1955, Lajos suffered a slipped disk and had to have surgery. It was successful. One day he told me about a job opening at the Komlo Coal Mine, which would be a good job for me to have so that we could secure income. The job was taking care of the lights on the hard hats, cleaning them and recharging the batteries for the miners. I went to work in the summer of 1955 while Lajos was in recovery. I became the breadwinner of the family. Later after Lajos healed, he started work in the mine with my niece, Eta Suhajda.

In 1956, the rumbling started, and Hungary was in complete turmoil. Lajos was approached to enter politics and run for Mayor of Godisa. He sat in on a couple of meetings to think about the offer. After researching many events happening in Hungary, he came to the realization that many members were not to be trusted. They were devout Communists, and his distrust for the Russians led him to suggest keeping the current politicians. The committee then asked him to be a guard for the City Council, and they wanted him to carry a gun. He turned all of the requests down that were offered to him.. If he had taken the Mayor position or the City Council guard job, it could have resulted in the execution of his life by the Communist Party.

Lajos' thinking was that if the Revolution was violently defeated, then he would be singled out for holding a gun, and then be accused of being a member of the Freedom Fighter group. Those Hungarians who were caught were either executed or deported to Siberia. The totality of events in his life brought him uncertainty about the future.

He would be judged on previous blacklistings and firings because he was not a card-carrying Red Book Communist,

Having been tried on false accusations of stealing fuel, plus regarding his family history and confrontations with the Communist Government, Lajos' point of view was that the children would also be discriminated against, and the boys may not get the same educational opportunities as other children. Religious persecution was ever so present in his mind, knowing the Secret Police were writing down names of attendees in church, in order to arrest them for their beliefs.

All this weighed heavily on his shoulders, and he knew he had to do something. So, with a heavy heart in despair, his final decision was to escape with his family from Hungary, the country he loved, and establish freedom for a better life.

Lajos' thoughts were about the missed opportunity that happened at the end of WWII, when he was offered an opportunity to refugee into the United States, but turned it down. There was now no future, only fear and oppression, with no hopes or dreams for the future. During this time, my father, Matyas Menrath died. I was devastated because he had been our security through all the hard times and a source of direction. It was November 12, 1956, and our world was coming apart.

A family meeting was called by Lajos, and everyone attended. The discussions of the future were the main topics, and Lajos remembered the American soldier's comments of starting a new life in America. All were in attendance: My mother, Anna, my sister, Nuci, her husband, Janos Vass, Lajos's brother, Pista Suhajda, his daughter, Eta Suhajda, and my brother, Feri Menrath. Tragedy engulfed everyone with sadness, uncertainty and resentment toward Russia's actions. Lajos announced, "We are escaping Hungary into Austria to start again in America. There are many reasons why we need to leave. I have been blacklisted because of Communism in this country, and I have struggled to support my family with odd jobs. I was given a wonderful position as an airport manager, only to have it taken away while on medical leave due to a false accusation against me. Even though I was exonerated in that case, I was still fired because I was not a Red Book Communist Party carrier. When I worked for the forestry company as a driver and a mechanic, I was fired because a truck driver did not announce his arrival and returned his lumber truck behind the building while I was draining the water out of the radiators for the fleet of trucks in the front of the building. And due to the freezing temperatures outside, it cracked the truck's block. Then I was assigned a job in the coal mines. I am an aviator! My hopes and dreams are just that, and all I get from these tyrants is "Het, NO!" My children, my wife and I do not have a future here in Hungary. The Communists will blacklist them too! They will not get the education that they deserve, and my boys need to live free. The only thing that has kept me going is all of you, my family. But, my decision is to escape. I choose freedom!"

There was a flurry of expressed emotions with everyone talking over each other.

I asked everyone to calm down so that everyone could voice their opinion. I started by saying, "I know the reports at the border from Radio Free Europe.[23] Many families are being arrested, and many families are being killed. The dangerous journey ahead is for adults, not children! (I started to tear up.) I would not forgive you or myself if anything happened to the children. I could not live with that." Feri spoke up, "Iren is right! It has been fifteen days since the Revolution ended. The borders are sealed by now. The chances of your escape meeting with tragedy are high." Nuci followed, "I agree with Feri. It is too dangerous! You must think of the welfare of the children." Janos

---

[23] Radio Free Europe had been broadcasting into Hungary since its creation in 1949, created in part by the United States CIA along with other nations in Western Europe who feared the spread of Communism.

added, "Train communications are reporting that it is a very dangerous time. The Russians are making a point to be as brutal as possible to strike fear into Hungarians in order to control the population. Innocent people and children will die. Do not do this!" Pista looked at Lajos and said, "I know you very well, and what I say will not matter. As you know, I also lost my big brother József, who perished in a Russian Prisoner of War Camp. I know how angry you are about his death, but there is nothing that can be done to change what happened. Your boys deserve a chance in life." Eta walked over to Pista and whispered in his ear. Anna, my mother, spoke while crying, "I just lost Matyas last week, and now I may lose my dear daughter and grandchildren. They may be killed during the escape. I am scared for them. Let Jozi, Bela, and Laci grow up in Hungary. Things might change here for the better. I can't live without my dear loved ones. Please don't go!" Mom was hysterically sobbing so much that Feri had to settle her down. Feri, Mom and I hugged with breaking hearts about the near future. Feri, consoling Mom, said, "Mom, you come home with me tonight."

Matyas Menrath died Novembe 12, 1956, eight days before our escape.

There was no arguing with Lajos, and truly everyone knew that. His decision was final. As everyone started to leave Mom's house, Pista came up to Lajos and pulled him aside then said, "Please take Eta, (his daughter), with you. She is fourteen years old and wants a chance for a future. She knows the danger but believes in the journey." When my mother left to go home with Feri, Lajos announced to Iren, "We are packing and leaving in the morning!" I packed all the children's clothes that night and got ready for our departure. Eta had lived with us since the summer because she was also working in the Komlo Mine. Lajos told Eta, "You need to go into the bedroom to pack your clothes to return to your parent's house. You will not be able to live here anymore, and unfortunately, it means that you will lose your job in the mine. The security of your parents is what you need." She watched us pack and boldly stated, "I want to go with you. I know the dangers and believe freedom is the best choice for me. Please take me! Please!"

Eta Suhajda photograph, Home photo.

Lajos and I looked at each other, and Lajos replied, "OK, go and pack, we leave at 5:00 a.m. while it's still dark."

So, at 5:00 a.m., November 20, 1956, we awoke, got dressed, and Lajos and I put black armbands on our coats as a symbol of a death within our family. It symbolized the death of my father, Matyas, who died November 12, 1956. We left Mom's house and started to walk toward the railroad station. We walked past Feri's house quietly, and my heart was breaking, knowing that I would not see Mom again. I could not control the tears as they ran down my cheeks.

We waited for the train at the Bakoca-Godisa railroad station. We boarded the train headed for Pecs at 6:30 a.m. and went to our first stop, Pecs. We arrived in Pecs and checked at the information desk. We asked, "When is the next train heading north toward Sopron arriving?" The information agent replied, "We don't know because of the Revolution and the nationwide strike affects all travel. As we receive information, we will announce it on the loudspeaker." We waited until 3:30 p.m. at the Pecs Train Station. We were being watched by the Secret Police, who would come up to us and ask, "Where is your destination? Why are you traveling?" One after another question was asked to us. It was very stressful, and we knew that if we cast suspicion, our journey would end immediately. Our plan was to travel from Pecs to Barc, Nagykanizsa, Zalaegerszeg, and then on to Szombathely with the final destination to Sopron-Peresteg. We decided on a story to tell if we were questioned. We were going to tell them that we were headed to our grandmother's house, who lived in Szeldemolk, a village outside of Sopron.

The constant questioning got us thinking that perhaps we were bringing suspicion upon ourselves with the black armbands. The Secret Police may be thinking that we had a relative who was a Freedom Fighter, and we were going to the funeral. I turned to Lajos and said, "We should take the armbands off, so we do not draw suspicion." Lajos agreed, and we removed the armbands. Well, my suspicions were confirmed because the attention subsided.

The announcement finally came over the loudspeaker that a train would be departing in the evening at 6:00 p.m. to Barc. We boarded the train and settled in for a long journey. The train stopped at every village and city with a twenty-minute wait at each stop. As we arrived in Szigetvar, we heard an announcement, "There will be a lengthy delay in travel. It has been reported that a stretch of tracks headed to Barc was mined, and a mine sweeper loaded with sandbags has been dispatched, in order to continue with safe travel." So, we waited an hour, and the mine sweeper returned with the good news that the tracks were clear and open for travel to Barc. At midnight, we boarded the train. The children slept in our arms. I held Laci, Lajos cradled Jozsef, and Eta had Bela sitting in her lap. The boys were all sleeping as the train departed for our journey toward our escape. When we arrived at Barc Station, there was no place to sit or lay down, in order to rest or sleep because it was packed with travelers. The boys were able to camp out on the floor and get some sleep. Around 3:00 a.m., the Secret Police came into the station and checked everyone's identification cards and ticket destinations.

In the morning, November 21st, we boarded our train and headed to Nagykanizsa, arriving there at 10:00 a.m. We went to the lobby to wait for the next train heading north to Zalaegerszeg. We were frustrated because of all the travel delays. We discussed the trains' reliability and decided to continue to Zalaegerszeg. But if the trains continued on this unpredictable track, we would end our journey and take the kids back home to Godisa. The three-hour sleep for the boys was enough to activate their hyperactive qualities. Laci was running around the lobby and upsetting the travelers who were trying to sleep. They complained about the children's actions. Lajos was angered and frustrated about the complaints and told me, "Iren, take the children and go back to Godisa. I will continue and check the route for safety and then come back for you." I was direct and replied, "No! We have come this far, and I am not going back just to start all over again!"

Finally, the announcement came to board the train to Zalaegerszeg. There was no interruption in this leg of the trip, and we arrived in the late morning. Much to our surprise, the train going to Szombathely was there, ready for us to board. We boarded the train and departed at 1:00 p.m. The train was not direct to Szombathely, and as a result, it made many unscheduled stops: Zala, Egerszeg, Szentmihaly and three other villages, which then returned to Szentmihaly with a direct passage to Szombathely. On our journey we passed the Zalai Gerszeg region where we saw the Russian tanks along the border all lined up with barrier fencing and land mine burying equipment.

We arrived in Szombathely on the evening of November 21, at 7:20 p.m.. Many of the passengers who were leaving Hungary got off the train. As we detrained, we were herded into two lines by the Secret Police for interrogation. They were collecting information from travelers in trying to catch anyone who may be trying to leave the country. We were in line: Lajos, József and Eta were together, and Bela and Laci were with me. We were going to use our story, that we were going to Sopron to visit our grandmother. The Secret Police called Lajos over to the left table just as I bent down to Laci with a handkerchief to blow his nose. As a result, there was a hesitation that followed, and the Secret Police on the right table called the boys and myself over. This caught me by surprise, and the officer immediately started asking questions in an authoritative manner. I went blank on the story line. He asked, "What are your names?" I answered, "My two sons are Bela and Laci Suhajda, and I am their mother, Iren Suhajda." He wrote down the answers in his book, and then he asked, "Where are you traveling to?" I knew I had to answer promptly and not show any fear. So, I replied, "We are going to visit my parents in Szekesfehervar." As soon as I said it, I knew that I made a mistake. I should have said, "in Sopron" to visit their grandmother. The officer said firmly, "What is the reason for your trip?" I replied, "Vacation trip so the boys can visit with their grandparents." He continued, "I need your identification card." I gave him my government identification. He looked at it, and then he looked at me and said, "Alright, you can go. Next person in line!" It appeared to me that he believed we were not connected with Lajos, József and Eta.

As we exited the train station, we saw an elderly lady from the train waiting for her family to pick her up. As we caught her eye, she waived, and we went over to her. She invited us to her daughter and son-in-law's farm for the evening. They lived one mile from the train station. She reported, "Tomorrow morning the Secret Police will be interrogating travelers once again. If you stay in the lobby at the station, they will be watching you and asking more questions that could lead to a dangerous situation. Please stay with us and board the train tomorrow morning to avoid the danger." We happily accepted her kind invitation, and a two-horse drawn wagon came to pick us all up at the station.

Eta and the boys slept in one bed, and Lajos and I slept on a carpet on the floor with blankets. Bela was the lucky one with the sleeping arrangements because the daughter of the elderly lady thought Bela was adorable, and so she put him into her bed.

The next day on Thursday, November 22, we woke up at 6:00 a.m. to a dark chilly morning. We got ready to leave when our host pointed out that they had never seen refugees leaving with so many suitcases as we had. They recommended that we repack and cut the number of suitcases from six down to four cases. That was extremely hard!

The train was scheduled to leave at 8:00 a.m. for Sopron. We boarded the train, and we discussed amongst us how we would know when to get off the train. Which station was the best and safest? Lajos told me, "I will ask the conductor and let him know what we are planning." I replied in a nervous voice, "You know, if he is a Communist, he will have us arrested, and who knows what will happen to us, especially the children!" Lajos thought for a moment and decided, "I will ask him, and perhaps he will help us." When the conductor came to stamp our tickets, Lajos had a friendly discussion with him. They talked about the nice weather that morning and how busy the train was. The conductor was friendly, and he explained how the train was the only source of travel because of the nationwide strike. Lajos decided to take the chance, and he told the conductor our plans to cross the border. The conductor paused and looked at the children and me. He paused again, then turned to Lajos and, talking in a whisper, said, "Yes, I will help you. I will get off at all the upcoming stops and ask the status of the

Russian troops in the area. I will give you a signal. If I take my hat off and rub the band to remove sweat, that is your signal to detrain. If I do not give you the signal, then we will continue to Sopron. If the Russian troops have secured the border, you will have to return home. We stopped along the way at seven villages. Every time we came to a stop, we stood up in anticipation while watching the conductor. He would get off and check in with the office, then he would return to the train with no signal.

We arrived at Sopron which was our last chance to escape. The conductor got off the train and checked with the office, as we were so concerned about the final outcome of our journey! As we were looking out of the window, the conductor took his hat off and rubbed his hat band. We hurried to collect all of our our things and luggage, and we proceeded to exit the car to detrain. The conductor met us at the steps and helped us off the train saying, "Take your time. There is no hurry." I took the boys to the crossing gate, while Lajos thanked the conductor and gave him all the money we had because Hungarian currency was worthless outside of the country.

At the crossing gate, I saw a farmer with an oxcart pulled by a steer. He yelled out, "Would you like a ride?" I replied, "Yes, thank you!" He took our bags and put them in the hay-filled cart along with the boys. Then he turned and introduced himself, "Good morning, I am Mr. Molnar, a farmer next to the Austrian border. I introduced myself and the children to him. The train pulled out of the station, and the gate lifted. The steer started down the dirt road toward the forest. We were walking next to the cart because the steer could not pull the weight of everyone. Lajos caught up to us and asked, "Hello, where are you taking us?" The farmer looking over at Lajos said, "Good morning, I am taking you to the border." "No, we want to cross at night," replied Lajos. The farmer explained, "No, you don't want to do that because the Russians patrol at night, and the Hungarian border guards patrol during the day. The Hungarians are sympathetic, but the Russians are not. They shoot flares in the air and machine gun down anything that moves. You want to cross now! I am taking you to my farm on the western edge of the border which has a good crossing point, about 1600 meters to Austria."

As I walked next to the oxcart, I realized that I may never see my mother or family ever again. The thoughts started to make me tear up. I was never one to complain about life, but it seemed so unfair that suffering had become so normal and that tragedy was always nearby. I thought about a Hungarian family in Yugoslavia that were neighbors. They worked hard for their home but did not keep up with the laws. There was especially one critical law which stated that all landowners had to file their property deeds with the government. This was the law created when Hungary was divided up and redistricted due to the Trianon Treaty. * They had to be citizens of Yugoslavia by a designated date. The law was clear, and if you were an alien, you could not own land. When the authorities came to remove the family from their cherished home, the mother broke away, and with her arms outstretched plus anguish in her heart, she looked at her home for the last time. I witnessed this as a young girl, and I could not believe the injustice. I completely sympathized with her family. I knew now just how she had felt. Her world was ending, and through a simple act of desperation, she demonstrated her compassion and despair. My world was also at a crossroads. My world was my children, and I knew that if anything happened to any of them, I would never forgive Lajos or myself as long as I lived!

As Lajos was walking behind the oxcart, he thought of all the good, kind people who had helped us get to this point. He prayed to God to watch over us with every step on our way. He looked at the children and asked himself, "Do they know the dangers ahead? Did I prepare them properly? Will they meet the dangers and handle them appropriately, or will they succumb to fear and cry out, exposing our position and resulting in death to us all?" I was remembereing back to a Saturday evening on November 10th when Radio Free Europe was broadcasting the events at the Hungarian border. Jozi and Bela were listening with their dad when Laci walked into the candle-lit living room and asked, "What are you listening to?" Lajos told him, "Radio Free Europe to learn the news of Hungary. The man is telling the story of the border and how dangerous it is. Families are being killed because their children are crying from fear, and the Russians are shooting them." Laci replied, "I would be quiet so those Russians would never find us!" Perhaps the children were braver than Lajos believed. The truth would be known within the next few hours. Lajos realized that the date, November 22, was ironically, Thanksgiving Day in America. It would truly be a thankful day if freedom awaited our family at the end of this escape journey.

I looked around to memorize the countryside, and I realized what a beautiful fall day was right there in front of me. I watched the birds fly, the rabbits run and a deer grazing in the field.

The temperature was in the mid-forties. The sun was shining brightly, the leaves were multicolored and there was a faint rustling of them in the breeze. This was truly a day to remember, and I appreciated the scenery that God had painted. This was a chance to take it all in for a moment.

As we approached our turn next to a cornfield, the cornstalks were tall and thick and swaying in the wind. We heard a jeep engine ahead of us on the same dirt road. The farmer quickly snapped the reigns to speed up the steer, and we made the turn just seconds before the jeep roared by. We stopped, and not making any noise, we saw three Russian border guards drive up the dirt road. We continued, shielded by the 8-foot-high cornstalks when the farmer broke his silence, "I will take you past my house to the back of my property. You can walk through the forest to Austria." The farmer stopped his oxcart about fifty yards in front of the forest. The terrain was a field of majestic tall grass with a dark green forest line in front of us. The children climbed down from the hay wagon, and our 4 bags were removed and placed on the ground.

Sopron-Peresteg border, that the Suhajda family went through to Austria and freedom. Home photo taken for the video, Freedom Revisited on Youtube, Home photo.

We were now ready to head into the forest to the border. I walked over to Eta and asked, "How are you doing?" Eta replied, "I am afraid." "I know sweetie, so am I, but we have to be strong and not let the boys see our fear." I replied.

I called the boys together and asked them, "Can you be brave young men and be very quiet as we walk through the woods? The reason we cannot make a sound is because the Russian soldiers will hear us, and you know what they will do if they catch us." The children nodded, and with that I continued, "Let's say a prayer so God will watch over us during our time of need, OK?" We said the Lord's Prayer, and when we finished, I gave them all a big hug then said, "Come on children let's get ready to go."

Just as I stood up, I saw two soldiers coming over the hill about seventy yards east of us. I was devastated and cried out in fear, "Oh my God! Are they Russians? Lajos, are they Russians?" Lajos looked for a moment and answered, "I can't tell, they are too far away." The soldiers came closer and closer, and my heart pounded louder and louder. "What will happen now?" I asked myself. Laci and Bela ran behind me and hugged each leg with fear, as the soldiers came over the final hill towards the oxcart. The farmer blurted out, "I know these soldiers. They are Hungarians, Imre and Istvan, I will talk to them. I believe everything will be alright." The farmer walked over to the soldiers and greeted them, "Hello, gentlemen! How are you on this beautiful morning?" The soldiers looked at the farmer and Imre asked, "What is going on here?" The farmer answered, "This family wishes to leave Hungary and go to Austria. You can arrest them now, but you know what the Russians will do to them. Please help them by turning your heads and let them continue their journey." "Is this a political family?" asked Imre. "No! Heavens No!", answered the farmer. Istvan, the other soldier added, "Mr. Molnar, are you absolutely sure this family has no political connections?" The farmer responded, "Yes, absolutely sure!" Imre added, "A political family's escape would be noticed and investigated. Their escape could be traced back to you, and you know the danger that could result from an investigation like that. It would almost certainly be an execution for you." Molnar replied, "Yes, I know the dangers, and I know both of you. Would you turn a family of four children over to Russian assassins?" The soldiers looked at each other and then at us. They told Molnar that they wanted to discuss the situation amongst themselves. The farmer walked back to us and said, "I think everything will be alright." Lajos and I hugged the boys holding onto us, and Eta was hugging us as well. We did not speak; our fear was very evident as the soldiers glanced over at us while they talked. A few minutes went by, and then they walked over to us. Their machine guns stayed on their shoulders as they approached and stood in front of Lajos and me. Imre said, "We will let you go through the forest to Austria.

We will draw a map for you to follow. There are Russian patrols walking through the forest, so you will have to remain extremely quiet. The small children will need to keep quiet for around two hours. Do you think they can?" "Yes, they can," I replied. Imre stated, "Good, if they remain quiet, you will have a very good chance of making it. If they cry out, you may be killed. Do you understand?" "Yes!" answered Lajos. Imre took out his notebook and started drawing a map, "Enter the forest there," pointing to an open area at the center of the forest line. "This path will lead you forty yards to the west that connects to a path heading North. Try to avoid stepping on twigs and leaves because they will make noise. You will see several jeep roads, and so be careful crossing those paths. Keep in mind to look both ways and listen for approaching motor vehicles. When you reach the northern point of the forest, you will see a section of plowed earth which is safe. It was once a landmine field. The landmines have been removed by Istvan, myself, and our detachment. Lajos, always walk through the plowed sections, and have the family follow in your footsteps because we may not have gotten all the land mines. There are Russian snipers, so try to stay in covered areas. After the minefield, you will see a barbwire fence. Beyond the fence is Austria and freedom. If you are caught, you did not see us! Is that understood?" "Yes!" Lajos and I replied in unison. The soldiers held out their hands and said, "Good luck, and may God watch over your family." Lajos and I shook hands with the soldiers. then Imre and Istvan calmly walked away.

Imre Gonczy, boarder guard photo 1956, home photo.

Molnar, the farmer, walked over to us, and as he smiled, he extended his hand and said, "Good Luck! I know you can make it." I replied, "On behalf of my family, thank you so much!" The farmer exclaimed, "it was a pleasure to help such a fine family as yours. You have made an old farmer very happy on this beautiful morning." He shook our hands, and he added, "What a fine day for freedom!"

All the bags were collected, and we started our walk toward the forest entrance. As we reached the entrance, I knelt down and looked at the boys and said, "Please be as quiet as you can, my darlings. Any sound may bring the Russians." We entered the forest at 10:00 a.m., and immediately an eerie sense of danger was magnified by a ten-degree drop in temperature. The children were very careful not to step on leaves or twigs that lay in their path. The boys intensely watched the placement of their feet. The forest was very silent except for the crickets that continued their rhythmic call to the shadowed forest.

The jeep roads inside the Sopron-Peresteg Forest that the family had to cross to Austria. Home photo for the video "Freedom Revisited" video on Youtube.

Lajos led the way with Eta following. Then Jozi, Bela and Laci proceeded in a single file line. I followed Laci to help him and comfort him in case he should be frightened. I could see Jozi laboring with his medium-sized suitcase ahead of me. He was very careful not to make a sound as he periodically switched hands with the case. Bela was so focused on his surroundings that he stayed steadfast to the course and observed any movement. The answer to Lajos's question was clear, the boys were extremely brave and focused.

As Lajos carried his bag, he continually looked back to check on everyone. He noticed Eta and Jozi were laboring with keeping up, and I was tired myself. Lajos put his hand up, signaling to stop and rest. We had made the turn to the north and were making good time, so a rest was in order. We had stopped before a dirt roadway and heard an engine sound. Lajos made a signal to kneel behind the bushes as a border guard jeep went by. We waited a minute or so to see if there were any more additional jeeps on the road. Since we did not hear or see any vehicles, we got ready to cross the dirt road. Lajos found a three-inch-thick branch and collected the suitcases. He then placed two in the front and two in the back of the branch. He selected this branch because the branch stubs that were broken off protruded an inch outward to hold the cases from slipping off. He placed the branch on his right shoulder and signaled everyone to continue. We crossed the dirt road, one by one, looking both ways and running across. We continued, escorted by the sounds within the forest of birds, owls, crickets, and an occasional rabbit running from the path.

We had been walking for about forty-five minutes when we heard a loud rustling sound about twenty yards northwest of our position. Lajos quickly signaled everyone to hide in the brush next to the path. We quickly and quietly stepped into the brush and squatted down while peering ahead through the bushes to see the source of the noise. Our hearts were pounding as we hid quietly for the noise to pass. A few minutes later, which seemed like hours, we saw the reason for the noise. It was a deer walking on the path and foraging for food without a care in the world as it continued through the brush. What a welcome sight it was to see a deer instead of Russian soldiers!!! If it would have been soldiers, it could have been very detrimental to all of us. I checked the boys and smiled, placing my finger to my lips, reminding them to stay quiet.

Lajos checked every crossing path, and he peered down the dirt road, to

make sure that no guards were walking on patrol. Then we quickly crossed that path with a new sense of determination. The directions of the Hungarian soldiers, Imre and Istvan, were accurate. I remembered the farmer stating to cross in the daytime because the Russians patrolled at night. Perhaps we caught them on a shift change. Anyway, it seemed like we did.

Barbed wire fence barrier to Austria, Wikipedia.

We finally reached the plowed section of the forest, and Lajos signaled for us to stop. He continued forward to examine the area and saw all the unearthed area where he believed were the extraction points of the landmines. He came back and whispered to all of us as we grouped together, "I will lead the way, and everyone has to step in my footsteps all the way through." We all nodded yes. Lajos placed the pole with the luggage on his shoulder and took short steps as he led the way so we could all follow. We followed him, stepping in his footsteps until we reached the barbed wire fence. Lajos took the bags off the pole and slid the bags under the bottom row of the barbed wire fence. Then he hooked the barbed wire with the pole as he pushed down with his right foot. Then he lifted the next row of barbed wire, creating a gap to step through. We plodded on, one by one, through the fence. The children were scared and tired but were doing such a wonderful job.

The wild grass was waist-high, and the boys were walking through using a breaststroke motion. About twenty-five yards from the fence, Laci tripped and fell on top of a Hungarian man who had been shot and killed by a sniper while trying to escape. We all stared at our fellow countryman, with his eyes crossed, and a pool of blood under his head. Unfortunately, his journey ended in that field with no freedom from his oppressors. I was afraid Laci would cry seeing this, so I quickly picked him up and hugged him tightly saying, "It's all right. We are safe." I caressed his back to comfort him, and then we continued walking. I looked at Lajos, and he was shaking his head at the sight.

What we did not know at that time, was that only fifty yards away along the border, there were two Russian soldiers who spotted us. These were the snipers that had shot our countryman just hours before. One of the Russian snipers picked up his rifle, attached the scope and said loudly to his comrade, "How do you turn victory into defeat?" He looked through the scope and was zeroing in on us as the nearby church's noon bells started to ring. His comrade asked him, "How?" The Russian sniper yelled, "By killing the youngest child at the sound of the twelfth bell. They all will suffer defeat!" Then the church bell rang out its second strike.

I saw some fieldhands working at a farm ahead of us, and I yelled out, "We are in Austria! Lajos, we made it! We're in Austria!" So, we were so happy, jumping up and down. Then a worker in the field saw us and started to wave at us with his arms. He was also jumping up and down and started to run toward us about two hundred yards away, as the church bell sounded "three". I handed Laci off to Lajos. I could not make out what he was yelling, so I ran toward him as the bell sounded "four". The farmhand continued to run and yell. I was thinking that the worker was Austrian, but then why couldn't I understand what he was yelling, as the bell Tolled "five". I decided to stop so I would be in range to communicate with Lajos. The worker continued to run toward us and yelled as the church bell rang out "six". I could barely hear his voice, but I realized he was not Austrian, as the church bell sounded "seven". I continued to listen at the stroke of the eighth bell. I noticed his gesture of a downward motion, at the stroke of "nine".

The Hungarian border view into Austria, Wikipedia.

He was now about one hundred yards away, still running and yelling, as the bell sounded its tenth strike. The Russian sniper was still focused on us. The crosshairs were set and ready at the stroke of "eleven". I realized that the farm hand was Croatian, and he was yelling, "Get down! There is a sniper behind you!" I turned and yelled at everyone, "Get down, a sniper! Get down, a sniper!" The Russian sniper started to squeeze the trigger as the bell sounded out "twelve". We heard a shot! Everyone had ducked down, but I did not know if anyone was shot. I ran back yelling, "Is everyone OK? Please God protect us." As the sniper took his shot, his rifle was kicked up in the air by a Hungarian Soldier.

The two snipers looked up, and there was Imre Gonczy, who looked down at them and yelled, "Het!" (the Russian word for NO)

THE END

The ending of this story was recounted by Imre Gonczy who became Eta Suhajda's husband and a forever-lasting friend of the family.

References

House of Terror, Andrassy Ut, Freedom Fighter Bios (Jozsef, 2002)

Joseph Vecsey & Phyllis Schafly, Mindszenty the Man (Schlafly, 1972)

Life magazine, 1956 Hungarian Revolution Photos ((Photographer), 1956)

Wikipedia, Historical information online Encyclopedia

Laci and mom hugging, Aurora IL Home photo.

My mother, Iren Suhajda, believed our journey was blessed by God. She said, "There were too many coincidences. Seven strangers helped us. They all did what they thought was a small and insignificant act, but all those wonderful acts gave us our freedom. Survivors of tyranny should tell their stories to teach those who value freedom with an important lesson to never allow disasters of history to repeat themselves."

In 2018 we traced our escape from Barcs to Sopron and posted a Youtube video called "Freedom Revisited the Suhajda Story."

Iren Suhajda, reenacting our journey, "Freedom Revisited"

Laci (Les), Jozsef (Joe), Bela (Bill) taken in 1957.

Jozsef (Joe), Laci (Les), Bela (Bill)

AUTHOR'S BIO

After my family's escape from Hungary, on November 22, 1956, we were processed into a placement system for our final destination which was either Australia, Canada or the United States. My father, Lajos, chose the United States. We traveled on a ship called the General Haan, which took two weeks with our arrival in New York harbor. It was thrilling to witness the Statue of Liberty, the symbol of the Land of the Free. Our family boarded a bus, and we were transported to an Army Base called Camp Kilmer, where my father was interviewed for a profession that could be used for sponsorship. I celebrated my 5th birthday on February 2, 1957, at Camp Kilmer. My family was sponsored by the Rotary Club in Ishpeming, Michigan, and we traveled by train to our destination. There was a big welcoming committee that met us when we arrived. My brothers, Bela and Jozef, were 7 and 9 years old. They were processed for elementary school along with Eta, my cousin, who was 14 years old and who also made this journey with us.

My father found a position at Austin Western in Aurora, Illinois. We moved there, and that is where I attended Brady Elementary School. My drive to fit into my new environment found athletics as my vehicle. I watched my brothers and learned from them. I excelled in football and basketball as a youngster. One day my father took my brothers and me to watch a soccer match with the Aurora Kickers team, and after the match, we asked to join the club. I practiced with my brothers and learned quickly how to envision each play of the game. When I became "of age" to play in the Juvenile age group, the 14-year-old division, I dominated and scored on a consistent basis. All through high school,

I played soccer, football, and wrestling. In my senior year, the Chicago Soccer Federation selected me for the Junior Olympics that was held in St. Louis, Missouri. Pat McBride, a St. Louis Stars professional soccer player, was my coach. It was a special time with fond memories.

In 1971, at Aurora College, I had the privilege of playing soccer with my brother, Bela (Bill). It was a recruiting year under Coach Bornkamp. Bill had told Coach Bornkamp about me, and he thought if I was close to Bill's talent, it could help the team. Bill and I led the team to a Division Championship, and through a team effort, I set a school scoring record that still stands today, of 22 goals and 8 assists in 14 games. One day, my East Aurora Varsity Assistant Coach, Coach Gavoni saw me walking to the commons and flagged me down to tell me that he was the new Aurora College Varsity Wrestling Coach. Then Coach Gavoni stated that he wanted me to join the team. I respected Coach Gavoni, and I couldn't say no. I was very successful at my 142 LB division, winning the Conference, District Championship, and four Tournament Championships. This all led me to qualify for the N.A.I.A. Nationals. I was the only Aurora College wrestler to ever accomplish that record.

As I was going into my sophomore year of college, I was drafted by the US Army. I thought about the family and how we were received in a free country. So, I enlisted in the US Navy in the fall of 1972. After "A" School, I was given orders to transfer to the Naval Air Station in Meridian, Mississippi. I worked in supply support and continued my soccer with the base team. My Commanding Officer sent me to Catonsville Maryland for the 1976 US Olympic Trials, and I made it through three rounds of trials until I was cut.

When I received military leave, I went home to be with my parents, and I taped their story from 1942 to 1956, which led to the writing of this book, "Twelve Bells to Freedom."

I met my wife, Elizabeth Ziegler, in the US Navy. We met in the barracks courtyard of Naval Air Station, Meridian, Mississippi. She transferred to Washington DC for duty, and that began our long-distance relationship. I was Honorably Discharged in March, 1976, and I flew to Arlington, Virginia to stay with my fiancé, Beth. I stayed for two months and returned to Aurora College to work on my degree. I transferred to SIU-E with a double major in Business Administration and General Accounting. Beth received her Honorable Discharge from the U.S. Navy in 1977 and continued with the Military Reserves at Lambert Field in St. Louis, Missouri. We were then married on September 9, 1978.

I graduated and went to work at McDonnell Douglas Corporation as a Senior Buyer of aviation parts for fleets of fighter jet planes. I worked there for eleven years until 1991. During that time my daughter, Laura, was born in 1980, and then my son, Mathew came along in 1983. I was a hands-on dad with sports in coaching soccer, baseball, and basketball. I worked for Chemisphere Corporation and was the purchasing manager for eleven years until 2002. I then decided to establish my own business, and I started a chemical distribution company called Laszlo Corporation. Later on, I opened another division that involved importing wines from Hungary. It is called Menrathwines. My wine business created a new frozen wine drink called Wine Slushee, which is very popular today.

In 2018, I entered into a green technology project, a wildfire remedy, that protects, retards, and suppresses fire. It is safe for people, animals, and the environment with no forever chemicals like PFOS or PFAS.

It is called Komodo K500C, approved by USDA, and it is on the Federal Register QPL. In November 2023, Komodo 911 spray suppressant cans rolled out using the same K500C formulation to extinguish fires in their infancy with the press of a button. USDA Forestry approved Komodo K500C, and it is available through my company, Laszlo Corporation.

I also started writing my family's story in 2018, "Twelve Bells to Freedom", and I finally completed the book in November of 2023. This is a life's journey from my parents to you.[24]

I started coaching my son, Mathew, and I continued to coach select soccer. My Real WC Freedom Team merged with the Lou Fusz Red Star Questra Team. Our combined Real Freedom and Questra Team had an impressive record from 2021 to 2023, winning nine Tournaments and League Championships. Our Lou Fusz Red Star Questra Team won the Jr. Champions Tournament, pictured below in November 2023.

---

[24] Pictures of Laszlo and Beth over the years. Out and about with friends, and a guest Wedding photo.

My wife, Elizabeth Ziegler Suhajda, joined the U.S. Navy in 1974 when she was 18 years old. After boot camp, she went to "A" School in Meridian, Mississippi, and she became a Yeoman (Secretary) to the upper brass in Washington DC. Her duties were at the Bureau of Naval Personnel and the Pentagon. She has a Master of Education Degree from the University of Missouri, St. Louis with many accolades. She taught for 27 years in the Ritenour School District, touching thousands of children's lives from Kindergarten to Middle School. Beth and I are living out our "Golden Years "in Cottleville, Missouri.

My daughter is Laura Suhayda Koper. Her children are Nadia Koper, Carson Koper and Kaden Koper. Laura was born on March 27, 1980. She was involved in gymnastics and softball, and she was on the swimming team in high school. She attended college for a Medical Business Degree. She gave birth to her daughter, Nadia, in 2004. Nadia became an awe-aspiring soccer player on select teams. She is presently in college to earn her degree in Law. Laura continued her family with her son, Carson, in 2007. He is an excellent football player for his high school team. His passion is to join the military upon graduation. Kaden came along in 2010. He loves many sports, but his passion for the games lies in hockey and soccer. Kaden is presently playing select soccer for my Lou Fusz Red Star Questra Team. Laura has worked for several medical jobs in the billing departments.

She worked for an Independent Living Facility as the Director of Finance and Human Resources, and she is presently working for a Nursing Care Facility as the Business Manager.

My son is Mathew Suhayda. His children are Eleanor Suhayda and Edith Suhayda. Mathew was born on December 30, 1983. He was a true athlete with many awards in baseball, basketball and soccer. He was an exceptional soccer player on several select teams, and he was on his high school varsity team as well. After high school, he worked as a Production Assistant on a few films and projects. Mathew graduated from Lindenwood University with a degree in Mass Communications. He met his significant other, Melissa Dutcher, who had a nursing degree and managed a nursing facility. Their first child, Eleanor, was born on July 20, 2015. She loves crafting, swimming and playing soccer. Mathew and Melissa were blessed with Edith on March 1, 2017. She is a great little performer who dances and sings daily. Her passion lies in cheerleading. She presently attends a cheerleading academy. Mathew worked for many years at Centenne Corporation as a Product Manager/ Senior Business Systems Analyst. Presently, he works for Mastercard as the Lead Reliability Engineer. Melissa works presently as a Healthcare Consultant. Mathew and Melissa live in Wentzville, Missouri with their family.

L to R; Steven, Erin Quinones, Rose, Jozsef (Joe), Lauren, Adam, Front: Eric and Andrew.

My brother, Jozsef (Joe) Suhajda excelled with his education, sports and music. He loved to play the flute and organ. He played for the Aurora Kickers Soccer Club at the University of Illinois and Northern Illinois University. Joe Graduated from Northern Illinois University with a degree in Business Administration. He married Rose Schlee in 1974. Rose earned a PhD and was an Associate Professor in the College of Nursing at Rush University. Joe entered the business world and worked in sales/ engineering for a pump company until his retirement. Joe and Rose had two successful sons, Adam Suhajda and Steven Suhajda. Adam earned a Master's Degree in Technology Programming. He presently works at Aldi's Headquarters. Adam married Lauren Skeens, who enjoys her profession as a Nurse Practitioner. Adam and Lauren are proud parents of their twin sons, Eric and Andrew. Steven Suhajda served his country proudly in the United States Marines for five years. He graduated from Lewis College with a Bachelor's Degree in Aviation Security. He currently received a second degree in Nutrition.

L to R back: Brian Evans, Brenda, Bela (Bill), Brett, Front L to R; Stephanie and Audrey, Alyssa, Joanna.

My brother, Bela (Bill) Suhajda had wrestling and soccer blood running through his veins at a very young age. He started his soccer development with the Aurora Kickers Soccer Club. He was an outstanding midfielder and playmaker. His soccer career led him to Northern Illinois University with a transfer to Aurora College. Our partnering in 1971 created a magical season with a League Championship with Conference, District and NAIA Honors. Bill graduated from Aurora College in 1973 with a double major in Biology and Psychology. He started his teaching career at Waldo Elementary School, and then he accepted a position at East Aurora High School as a Science Biology Teacher. He coached wrestling and soccer for twenty-five years at East Aurora and retired in 2005. He married Brenda Shafer in 1977. Brenda graduated from Northern Illinois

University with a Teaching Degree and taught for six years as an Elementary School Teacher. Then she worked for several insurance companies until she retired. Bill and Brenda had two children, Stephanie and Brett. Stephanie graduated from North Central College with a Business Degree and works at Metropolitan Life Insurance Company as a Client Service Consultant. She married Brian Evans in 2010. Stephanie and Brian have two beautiful daughters, Alyssa and Audrey. Brian worked for the City Public Works Department. Brett Suhajda followed Bill's lead with the passion for wrestling and soccer. Brett graduated from Lawrence College with a Biology Degree and later obtained a master's degree at the University of Massachusetts with a Plant and Soil Science Degree. Bret presently works for ENCAP and is the Waubonsee Community College Soccer Coach. Bret married Joanna Schander in 2011. She works for Midwestern Contractors as a Billing and Accounts Manager.

L to R; Antonio, Mariann Suhajda Rojas, Marco, and Robert.

My sister, Mariann Suhajda Rojas was born in 1966, in Aurora Illinois. She is the first-generation family member born in the United States. My mother, Iren, got her wish, and she was pampered, spoiled, and loved by all of us! She was gifted with musical talents, which she expressed when she played the organ. She was also athletic, playing soccer, gymnastics, and cheerleading in high school at East Aurora. Mariann,

(Babi) is a college graduate from Waubonsee Community College with a Nursing Degree. She worked for Delnor Hospital as a Registered Nurse and then worked in a family practice office. She presently is a Nurse Care Manager, developing treatment plans for patients with their physicians. Mariann married Robert Rojas in 1995. Robert worked for Inland Mortgage as a loan officer. Then he worked for Harris Bank in the loan department. He studied at Aurora University. They had two sons, Antonio and Marco. Antonio graduated from Augustana College with a degree in Social Services and presently works in that field. Marco graduated with honors from the University of Illinois with an Engineering Degree, and he now works for Texas Instruments as a Field Applications Engineer. Marco married Alli Pfister in 2023.

My cousin, Eta Suhajda escaped Hungary with us in 1956 during the Revolution. She met Imre Gonczy, who was the Sopron Hungarian border guard who helped us with directions to the border of Austria. Imre escaped Hungary the week after my family crossed the border on November 29, 1956, and he refugeed to the United States. Ironically, they met again in Aurora, Illinois. They fell in love and were married on January 2, 1960. This proves how small the world is! They had two sons, Imre Jr., and Steve, plus one daughter, Clara. Clara Gonczy married Bruce Coleman, and they adopted a daughter, Jennifer. She recently married John Simon. Eta passed away on June 8,

Eta Suhajda Gonczy and Imre Gonczy

2008, and she stays in our hearts forever. Imre lives in Yorkville, Illinois, and he enjoys his family life with his children and granddaughter.

Iren Menrath Suhajda and Lajos Suhajda

My father, Lajos Suhajda, and my mother, Iren Menrath Suhajda came to the United States in search of a better life for my brothers, sister, and me. It was hard for all of us to initially function in society because of the language barrier. My parents worked very hard with various jobs to give us the best life possible. They paved the way for success in this new free world. They made sure that there was always food on the table and a roof over our heads. We felt loved and appreciated! Father and Mother were our heroes. They brought stability to our childhood and a source of strength to the entire family. It was the little things they did that put the finishing touches on every experience. They taught us to get back up again when things got tough. Even though they loved their new lives in the United States, their hearts yearned for their motherland of Hungary and the loved ones that they left behind. So, when the Iron Curtain fell in 1989, their roads led them back to the place that gave them peace and purpose. They are both buried in the Hungarian soils of their ancestors before them. Their final journeys brought them serenity and rest in their beloved country. My father, Lajos Suhajda passed away on September 6, 2010, and my beautiful mother, Iren Menrath Suhajda took the hand of our Lord on February 16, 2019. As they entered God's paradise, the neighboring church bells rang out for them one last time…For now, they were truly free!!! Father and Mom will always be remembered as beacons of light in our lives. They are truly missed and stay deep within our hearts.

www.ingramcontent.com/pod-product-compliance
Lightning Source LLC
Chambersburg PA
CBHW050650160426
43194CB00010B/1877